SPIRITUAL CARE REFLECTIONS FROM A HOSPICE CHAPLAIN

REV. CHARLES J. LOPEZ, JR.

Energion Publications
Gonzalez, FL 32560
2015

Copyright © 2015, Charles J. Lopez, Jr.

Scripture quotations are from the New Revised Standard Version Bible, copyright © 1989 National Council of the Churches of Christ in the United States of America. Used by permission. All rights reserved.

Cover Photo: Charles J. Lopez, Jr.
All interior photographs are by the author.

ISBN10: 1-63199-218-X
ISBN13: 978-1-63199-218-6
Library of Congress Control Number: 2015954122

Energion Publications
P. O. Box 841
Gonzalez, FL 32560

energion.com
pubs@energion.com
850-525-3916

Words to Begin ...

The round *Rose Window* is from the Sacred Heart Chapel on the campus of the Sisters of St. Joseph Community, Orange, California

Be at peace with yourself first and then you will be able to bring peace to others ...
— Thomas à Kempis, priest and probable author of *The Imitation of Christ*

[The LORD said,] *"Do not fear, for I have redeemed you; I have called you by name, you are mine."*
— Isaiah 43:1, prophet of the Old Testament

We are all one.
— Lakota Prayer, indigenous people (tribes) of the Great Plains of North America

To be what we are, and to become what we are capable of becoming, is the only end of life.
— Robert Louis Stevenson, Scottish novelist and poet

*The LORD is my shepherd, I shall not want ...
surely goodness and mercy shall follow me all the days of my life, and I shall dwell in the house of the LORD forever.*
— Psalm 23:1,6

When the heart weeps for what it has lost, the soul rejoices for what it has found.
— Sufi Proverb, Muslim movement

If you want to lift yourself up, lift up someone else.
— Booker T. Washington, educator and author

DEDICATION

*To Nancy Lou Klemme, my wife and
Wilma Pauline Lopez née Steinhauer, my mother.
Both received hospice care.*

Picture Locations and Notes

All photographs are by the author.

Cover – Cul-de-Sac, East South Street, Anaheim, CA
i – Rose Window, Sisters of St. Joseph
3 – Nancy Lou Klemme at Sakura Finetek Office, Torrance, CA
6 – Oceanside, CA
9 - Inside home
13 – Oceanside, CA
19 – Las Vegas, NV
21 – Oceanside, CA
23 – Oceanside, CA, Mission Bell (Mission San Luis Rey)
26 – Oceanside Pier
28 – Sedona, AZ, Chapel of the Holy Cross
32 – Outside home
35 – John Wayne Airport, Santa Ana, CA. John Wayne Statue
37 – Rose, front yard, home
39 – Bird of Paradise, backyard, home
40 – Butchart Gardens, Victoria, British Columbia
45 – Orthodox Church, Las Vegas, NV (outside); St. John the Baptist Greek Orthodox Church
48 – Orchid – inside home
49 – Gardens, Sisters of St. Joseph of Orange, Orange, CA
50 – End of East South Street, Anaheim, CA
53 – Light House, Rancho Palos Verdes, CA. Point Vicente Lighthouse
55 – Orthodox Church, Las Vegas, NV (outside)
57 – Backyard, home
59 – Sewer cover, Hermosa Beach, CA
62 – Orthodox Church, Las Vegas, NV
64 - Rose Window from Community Congregational UCC, Los Alamitos, CA
65 – Morning, Lake Tahoe
66 – Blessing of the hands
69 – Kiel, Wisconsin, Sheboygan River
72 – Lake Louise, Alberta, Canada (Banff National Park)
77 – San Clemente Pier, San Clemente, CA
79 – Madonna & Child by Sister Jeanne Fallon, Sisters of St. Joseph of Orange, CA
81 – Gardens, Sisters of St. Joseph of Orange
120 – Columbia Ice Fields/Glacier…Continental Divide, British Columbia/Alberta
121 – The author and St. Luke painting. Painting by Miriam Patrick, St. Luke's Lutheran Church, Fullerton, CA

Table of Contents

Words to Begin … i
Introduction 1

Reflections

1. A Chaplain's Grief Reflections 3
2. A Day of Remembrance 6
3. Bereavement Support: For the Front Line Workers.......8
4. Manhattan Beach Volleyball … Can you Dig it? 12
5. A Journey This Grief 15
6. Are You Worth It? 19
7. Summer Sabbath 21
8. Tears and Death at the US/Mexican Border 23
9. Where Angels Fear to Tread 26
10. Humor? Oh Yes! 28
11. The Mourner's Code 32
12. The Bronze Boot 35
13. Remembrance and Transformation:
    An Evening with Thich Nhat Hanh 37
    A Morning and Afternoon with the Dalai Lama 39
14. Spiritual Presence During Parathyroid Surgery...........40
15. It's What's Inside that Counts! 45
16. A Silent Retreat and the Missing Thumb 48
17. Have You Seen the Light? 50
18. Will the Real Charley Chaplain Please Stand Up! 52
19. The River is Wide and the Water is Cold or
    A River Gathering 53
20. Greek Orthodox Church 55
21. "Walk as children of light …" 57
22. Don't Blow Your Sewer Cover! 59
23. Ecumenical Partners 62
24. Door to Paradise..65
25. Blessings

	No Two Hands Are Alike 66
	Blessing of the Home 69
26	A Chaplain's Grief Reflections: Two Years Later 72
27	The Puddle Fish 77
28	Madonna With Child 79

Appendixes

A	Decisions at the End of Life, Part 1 83
B	Directives for End of Life 86
C	The Affordable Care Act 89
D	Elder Abuse 93
	More Resources 95
	Author Biography 121

Introduction

Hospice has been around for a long time. Hospice implies hospitality. It is possible to trace hospice care back to fourth century Rome, when it was reported that a woman named Fabiola used her own wealth and personal effort to care for the sick and dying. The early hospices in Europe provided shelter and lodging for travelers. In addition, early hospices also addressed the needs of the sick, suffering, and dying. Hospice was introduced to the United States in the early 1960's. The names Elizabeth Kübler-Ross and Dame Cicely Saunders, both physicians, immediately come to mind in their care for the dying and introduction of hospice principles. The Irish Sisters of Charity, St. Christopher's Hospital, London, where Cicely Saunders served, and Yale–New Haven Hospital were in the forefront of the hospice movement. The Congress of the United States of America recently voted to extend Medicare coverage to hospice care (mainly because it is less expensive than hospitals or nursing homes).

Hospice Spiritual Care

What does a spiritual care provider do? A spiritual care provider offers "presence" of the Holy One to the hospice patient, their families and loved ones. Since hospice serves people with various religious and spiritual backgrounds, the spiritual care provider needs to be a good listener. Spiritual care providers ask before doing. Making assumptions is what can cause the individual and family much grief and give the chaplain another "black eye." Frequently people do not want to see the chaplain "until it's time …" Sometimes individuals need time to work on their end of life issues. The spiritual care provider also makes contact with the leaders in the spiritual community. Church, synagogue, mosque, temple, all sacred places of worship are honored and respected. The spiritual care provider in consultation with the individual and or family contacts religious/spiritual leaders and makes arrangements for visits from them to occur.

The Hospice Team

The hospice team consists of a medical director/physician, usually trained in palliative care; nurses; social workers, chaplains; home health aids; dietitians; physical therapists; volunteers, etc. A hospice organization may also be connected with a local hospital/medical center. Some hospices have Foundations where millions of dollars are raised and support is given beyond the Medicare benefit.

Spiritual Care Reflection

The following reflections serve as a guide to spiritual care with individuals and families who have received or are receiving hospice care. Spiritual care includes care for the entire person in mind, body, and spirit. By the same token, hospice is not only clinical, it is physical as well as spiritual. To neglect the spirit is to miss the presence of the Holy. The purpose of these reflections is to stimulate your thoughts and feelings as you approach hospice care for yourself or for someone you love. God grant you peace in your journey.

REFLECTION 1

A CHAPLAIN'S GRIEF REFLECTIONS

My wife, Nancy, died one month ago (January 3, 2012). She had planned to return to work teaching other histologists on the techniques of using the laboratory equipment made by Sakura Finetek or troubleshooting in local hospitals with her histology background. Her diagnosis was colon cancer with metastases to the liver and lungs. Nancy endured two years of chemotherapy and had two weeks of radiation treatments three weeks before she died. Nancy was independent and even a bit stubborn as she continued to pay bills up to January 2nd! I learned the other day that the mortgage was paid through the month of February. She did however, forget to pay the Orange County taxes!

Everything is so green in Southern California in the winter. When you drive along the freeways the beautiful vibrant colors meet you: the purples, reds, bright yellows and oranges. The birds of paradise flowers go wild and the hills around the Los Angeles basin are as green as they can be. You can always count on the snow being on the top of the mountains!! The ocean surf is ready for surfers even in the Winter. Nancy loved flowers and our house is bursting with lots of flowers, thanks in part to the green thumb of my mother-in-law, Sally. Sally *"loved to put her hands in the dirt"* as she would say. Both Sally and Nancy had deep roots in the small Midwestern town of Kiel, Wisconsin, not far from Sheboygan, which is on the western shore of Lake Michigan. Nancy was born at St. Nicholas Hospital, Sheboygan and even attended a one room school for grades 1-3 in neighboring Schleswig County.

After twenty years of marriage, twenty-five, if you count all the dating, I miss Nancy. The most difficult experience has been the commute into Torrance and the return trip to Anaheim. We commuted together for ten years, traveling the 91 Freeway in the carpool lane. Now I see Nancy's empty seat and the tears begin to flow. It has been that way for a month and I would imagine the tears will continue for many more months. The memories are good! We would share our work day, the good, bad and sometimes ugly. We enjoyed listening to KUSC-91.5 FM and would comment on the classical music we heard. We enjoyed Dennis Bartel in the mornings from 5 am when he would say, *"Good morning it's 5 am, it's a new day."* Dennis would go on with the weather, the traffic report and even a snooze alarm selection ... he would always bring a smile, especially when he would give the traffic report, saying *"Joe's Tow Truck has been called to the scene"* ... you could almost see Joe's toe, if you know what I mean!

My ministry as a hospice chaplain presents interesting challenges and opportunities for growth. I am especially sensitive and vulnerable when I visit patients who have a similar diagnosis as Nancy's, that is colon cancer. The other day a young woman, in her early 50's died from colon cancer and I was called upon to do the death visit. I listened and supported the husband who was grief stricken. When he said, "What am I going to do now?" I lost it. It was like having a mirror in front of me. I joined him in tears.

Whenever I hear *"Nearer My God to Thee," "It is Well with my Soul," "Borning Cry"* and Willie Nelson's *"Family Bible"* and *"Sweet Bye & Bye,"* the tears begin to flow. I have images of Nancy's faith and hope the last few weeks of her life. She loved the Lord and *"was ready to meet Jesus"* as she said. She witnessed to me about how she found the strength to move forward, not focusing on the hurt and pain, but on what was around the corner. She accepted what was happening and knew that she would die soon.

As the family came from Arizona, Wisconsin and other parts of the country, most stayed at a local Embassy Suites. By the way, they have the best manager's special in the evenings and the greatest breakfast in the morning. We would get together in the evening for stories and family togetherness. This started the healing process. Nancy would have loved the stories about the Kiel families and even the Chicago relatives! She would have loved the manager's evening specials as well!

Grief keeps rolling on and I plan to attend a local grief group and share my insights as well as struggles. I am thankful to have a spiritual director who has been helpful with my anticipatory grief. I have found Granger Westberg's classic, *Good Grief,* to be of great comfort. Another recent resource is *The Essential Guide to Grief and Grieving* by Debra Holland. Debra offers a practical, patient hand to hold as you travel the grief path. I miss Nancy and know that she is resting in God's eternal peace. May God grant me peace in my grief journey.

REFLECTION 2

A DAY OF REMEMBRANCE

No longer shall they teach one another, or say to each other, "Know the Lord," for they shall all know me, from the least of them to the greatest, says the Lord; for I will forgive their iniquity, and remember their sin no more.

— Jeremiah 31:34

Then he said, "Jesus, remember me when you come into your kingdom."

— Luke 23:34

The host for this Day of Remembrance (a Memorial Day weekend) said, "There are about 35 living veterans from World War I around the country ... one lives right here in Orange county and he is 103!" They, along with veterans from World War II, Korea, Vietnam, Iraq and other conflicts were remembered and honored on that day at the Annual Memorial Day service at Fairhaven Memorial Park and Mortuary, Santa Ana, California.

It was a day for pausing to remember those living and dead who have served in the Armed Forces. I carried my father's dog tags with me and held them high when the Navy song, *Anchors Aweigh*, was played. My father was a hospital corpsman stationed in Samoa during World War II. The chaplain helped us remember that peace and harmony are the ultimate goals of all of the wars and conflicts. Countless veterans bear the physical, emotional and mental scars of war.

There are disabled veterans in our midst today ... young men and women who bear the burden and reminders of war. Some continue to struggle with **post-traumatic stress disorder** (PTSD) like the 85 year old gentleman I visited on hospice living in Westchester. He struggles with how he survived while most of his buddies did not.

Learning to live in peace and harmony with all our brothers and sisters on this earth, regardless of their religious convictions, is indeed a mighty goal. Besides the globe continues to shrink and we are connected to all that God has created.

Reflection 3

Bereavement Support: For the Front Line Workers

Let love be genuine; hate what is evil, hold fast to what is good; love one another with mutual affection; outdo one another in showing honor. Do not lag in zeal, be ardent in spirit, serve the Lord. Rejoice in hope, be patient in suffering, persevere in prayer. Contribute to the needs of the saints; extend hospitality to strangers.

Bless those who persecute you; bless and do not curse them. Rejoice with those who rejoice, weep with those who weep. Live in harmony with one another; do not be haughty, but associate with the lowly; do not claim to be wiser than you are. Do not repay anyone evil for evil, but take thought for what is noble in the sight of all. If it is possible, so far as it depends on you, live peaceably with all. Beloved, never avenge yourselves, but leave room for the wrath of God; for it is written, "Vengeance is mine, I will repay, says the Lord." No, "if your enemies are hungry, feed them; if they are thirsty, give them something to drink; for by doing this you will heap burning coals on their heads." Do not be overcome by evil, but overcome evil with good.

— Romans 12:9-21

"Life gives us magic and life gives us tragedy, everyone suffers some loss. Till we have faith in it, childlike hope. There is a reason that outweighs the cost."
— *The Color of Roses*, words and music by Beth Nielson
BNC Songs, 1997.

Nurses, social workers chaplains, home health aides, volunteers and even physicians find time to grieve the people they have served. Each month the bereavement coordinator leads the team members in a time of remembrance.

We gather in an environment where candles are burning, music is playing, flowers of every size and shape fill the room with beauty, grace and good smells. There may even be a few scattered rose petals … one petal for each person who has passed.

On April 19, 2005 we were reminded and remembered that the world celebrated a new Pope, Pope Benedict XVI (Joseph Cardinal Ratzinger, from *Germany*!) Then on February 11, 2013, Pope Benedict announced that he would relinquish the Petrine ministry at the end of the month.

On March 13, 2013 another Pope began, the former Archbishop of Buenos Aires, Cardinal Jorge Mario Bergoglio, from Argentina, now Pope Francis! The first Jesuit Pope! And the first words of Pope Francis were, "Pray for me."

And now … we remember and pray for the people who entered and touched our lives. We remember:

» a husband who was a pediatrician.
» a social worker who said, "She always winked at all who visited."

- an answered request, " ... the ashes were taken back to New Jersey."
- one patient who was an avid wanderer and travelogue writer.
- she was a "professional polka partner and a fighter to the end."
- he was ... not connected to the church.
- she was "full of wisdom ... seeing angels and hearing 'swing low, sweet chariot ... '" and heard these words, "stop suffering and come with me."
- is your hair always that curly?
- she abused her son ... and now the son calls his mother, "a saint."
- "We come from where we go ..."
- trophies ... running ribbons in a room filled with local history.
- Visiting a member of the original Tuskegee Airmen who flew missions during World War II;
- one patient even knew the late Howard Hughes;
- there was this incredible long haul truck driver
- dentists, physicians, lawyers, lay rabbi, commercial fishermen, engineers, poets, skeptics, ship captains, military officers and foot soldiers, singers, oil tanker captains and crew members,
- those who knew the Big Band leaders like Tommy Dorsey, Artie Shaw, Benny Goodman, Glenn Miller, Jimmy Dorsey, Harry James, and even the young Frank Sinatra, Bob Eberly and Helen O'Connell, the Andrew Sisters, Harry Warren, Bing Crosby, Ella Fitzgerald, Count Basie, Erroll Garner, Lionel Hampton, Woody Herman, Charlie Barnet, Duke Ellington, Billie Holiday and Louis Armstrong;
- a cousin to the Pointer sisters,
- aerospace workers, dock workers, judges, shuttle engineers, Hughes aircraft designers, vaudeville actors and actresses, symphony members, car makers and designers, carpenters, contractors, chemists, secretaries, biologists, first grade school teachers, electricians, plumbers, a UCLA German professor, Buddhists, Hindus, atheists, agnostics, seekers, searchers, Muslims, Jews, Christians, Mormons, lapsed Catholics, editors,

writers for the *LA Times* and *Orange County Register*, radio announcers, marathon runners, photographers, surgeons, bankers, business men and women, hotel executives, several Disney designers, grandfathers, grandmothers, mothers, fathers, brothers, sisters, aunts, uncles, cousins, nephews, nieces,

» and yes, even Bill Sharman, Los Angeles Lakers coach who coached the Lakers when they won 33 straight NBA basketball games during the 1971-72 season

... the list is endless.

Through it all nurses, social workers, chaplains, and home health aids shed tears as people are remembered. Lives are touched and visions are opened. People make a lasting impression, even if you only see them once.

Their goal, their final wishes, physical therapy, comfort care, understanding glances, warm smiles, and laughter ... they all accompany the occasional tear and wish for God's mercy and compassion at this time in a person's life. Hospice ... the stories are endless and the journey keeps rolling along in the distance. Thank you for being there. The singing bell is heard in the distance ... names are spoken ... a life is remembered and tears are flowing. "... Everyone suffers some loss ..." and we remember.

The psalmist helps us remember that:

> *The Lord is my shepherd, I shall not want. He makes me lie down in green pastures; he leads me beside still waters; he restores my soul. He leads me in right paths for his name's sake.*
>
> *Even though I walk through the darkest valley, I fear no evil; for you are with me; your rod and your staff— they comfort me.*
>
> *You prepare a table before me in the presence of my enemies; you anoint my head with oil; my cup overflows. Surely goodness and mercy shall follow me all the days of my life, and I shall dwell in the house of the Lord my whole life long.*
>
> – Psalm 23

Reflection 4

Manhattan Beach Volleyball ... Can you Dig it?

Immediately he made his disciples get into the boat and go on ahead to the other side, to Bethsaida, while he dismissed the crowd. After saying farewell to them, he went up on the mountain to pray.

When evening came, the boat was out on the sea, and he was alone on the land. When he saw that they were straining at the oars against an adverse wind, he came towards them early in the morning, walking on the sea. He intended to pass them by. But when they saw him walking on the sea, they thought it was a ghost and cried out; for they all saw him and were terrified. But immediately he spoke to them and said, "Take heart, it is I; do not be afraid." Then he got into the boat with them and the wind ceased. And they were utterly astounded, for they did not understand about the loaves, but their hearts were hardened.

— Mark 6:45-52

The proposal pleased Pharaoh and all his servants. Pharaoh said to his servants, "Can we find anyone else like this [Joseph] – one in whom is the spirit of God?"

— Genesis 41: 37-38ff

The ball can be a blur ... the volleyball with sand and speed ... zipping right by you. From grade school to the pros, the sphere moves at great speeds and so do the players. Do you remember the volleyball companion of Tom Hanks while he was stranded on a remote island in the movie, *Cast Away*? The movie starred Helen Hunt and was directed by Robert Zemeckis.

Perhaps you have been one of the cheering spectators at a popular beach volleyball tournament or maybe you find yourself sitting in front of the television saying, "How did she dig that one?" People come to the beach to put their feet in the sand and rub elbows with the players. Beach volleyball was born in Southern California. You know its gotta be the beach, the sun, the ocean, the babes, the hunks, the Beach Boys music and oh yes, the flash of a flying ball ... they certainly get your attention on the beach.

In the 1960's a young man active with the Recreation Department of Manhattan Beach organized what would become the Manhattan Beach Volleyball Open. Charlie Saikley's name is synonymous with volleyball and people in Manhattan Beach know him and love him very much. He has been and continues to be the driving force behind the fast moving volleyball. As head of the Recreation Department in Manhattan Beach, he has organized many tournaments and launched the careers of current Association of Volleyball Professionals (AVP) players, males and females. (See www.volleyball.org or drop a line to the Volleyball Hall of Fame 171 Pine Street, Holyoke, Massachusetts 01040, 413-536-0926, volleyball's birthplace in 1895 at: info@volleyball.org.) Volleyball continues to be an Olympic sport.

Not long ago, Charlie was honored by the City of Manhattan Beach, with a plaque at the entrance to the Manhattan Beach Pier. His name is there embedded in the concrete walkway along with all the Manhattan Beach Volleyball Open winners: Charles "Karch" Kirarly, Sinjin Smith (Christopher St. John), Randy Stoklos, Ron Von Hagen, Misty May, Kerri Walsh, Holly McPeak, Elaine Youngs, Mike Lambert, etc. The plaque reads: *Creating another day in paradise since 1964 through volleyball & numerous sports ... Father of Manhattan Beach Open & 6 Man ... Charlie Saikley, Tournament Director, Presented August, 2003, Educator – Mentor.*"

While visiting Charlie, I noticed several large photos on the wall in his Manhattan Beach family room. There's an early photo of Karch Kirarly, spiking the volleyball ... a scene that would be repeated many times in Karch's career.

As a patient with Trinity Care Hospice, Saikley's dream is to visit the beach one more time, to see and feel the sand and breeze, hear the crowd, smell the ocean, and experience the love of his friends. His son, Jay, seems to have the drive to continue in his father's sandprints. The other day, Jay said, "it's going to be an exciting year ..." The beach is always open for Charlie Saikley ... or as they say in volleyball-ese, "Folks, the beach is officially open." God bless the Father of the Manhattan Beach Open!

REFLECTION 5

A JOURNEY THIS GRIEF

Haugk, Kenneth C. *Journeying Through Grief*. St. Louis, Missouri: Stephen Ministries St. Louis, 2004. ISBN: 1-930445-11-3. A Set of Four Books. Book One – A Time of Grieve; Book Two – Experiencing Grief; Book Three – Finding Hope and Healing; and Book Four – Rebuilding and Remembering. NOTE: each book is 40 pages. Giver's Guide, 16 pages.

Ken Haugk is a pastor, clinical psychologist, and founder of Stephen Ministries (materials for training caregivers in ministry settings). *Journeying Through Grief* utilizes Haugk's research team. They interviewed more than 100 grieving people, and surveyed more than 2,000 people about their grief experiences. He also included his own grief experience after losing his wife, Joan, to ovarian cancer in 2002.

A set of four books is given or sent (Giver's Guide, p. 3) to a grieving person at specific times during the first year of loss: *Book 1, A Time to Grieve* – three weeks after the loss, *Book 2, Experiencing Grief* – three months after the loss, *Book 3, Finding Hope and Healing* – six months after the loss, and *Book 4, Rebuilding and Remembering* – eleven months after the loss (so that it arrives a few weeks before the one-year anniversary of the loss).

Throughout these books Haugk shares examples from the bereaved and includes insightful quotes from the Scriptures, and other researchers in the field of bereavement.

Haugk says that there are *no magical words* to bring an end to one's pain. A person may be in shock, feel numb or they may feel as if they are in the fog. Much of the feelings may be of emptiness. Grief is a very **normal, natural, and necessary** process (3 N's, Book 1, p. 3ff). Grief is unique. Show your feelings … it's healthy and it shows you're human.

What affects your grief? Consider the following: loss of a parent, loss of a spouse, loss of a child, miscarriages, stillbirths, or infant deaths, and loss of a sibling. Don't forget the sudden versus anticipated death. In addition recognize the causes of death: an accidental death, a sudden death from natural causes, a death from a chronic or long-term illness, a suicide, or a murder. (Book 1, p. 16-21) "No, you're not going crazy. Crazy feelings are normal in grief" (Book 1, p. 10).

Earl Grollman, who has written and taught extensively in the area of grief asked Ken, *"What do you think is the worst kind of grief?"* The answer: *"your own grief"* (Book 1, p.14ff). A man who suffered multiple losses said, *"When you lose a parent you lose your past; when you lose a spouse you lose your present; when you lose a child you lose your future"* (Book 1, 16ff).

There are many **myths** about grief (Book 1, p. 31ff). Here are several: "People with a strong faith don't grieve." "Crying is a sign of weakness." "Only immediate family members will experience significant grief." "Getting angry at God or asking God difficult questions means you have a weak faith." "Grief proceeds through very predictable and orderly stages." Don't believe the myths, Haugk says, "they simply aren't true."

Likewise, there are many feelings of grief: panic or helplessness, worry or anxiety, fear, anger, guilt, failure, emptiness or hopelessness, despair or sadness, loneliness, relief, happiness (Book 2, p. 14-16).

He reminds grievers to take good care of themselves, meaning emotionally and physically (Book 1, p. 24ff). It's okay to cry and to let your emotions flow. After your loved one has died there will be a year of firsts. These "firsts" are significant and important: first birthday, first anniversary, first vacation, first holiday, etc. (Book 2, p. 25-26). These times can be emotionally charged.

I found the chapter on what other people say or do (Book 2, p. 35) to be significant. People may say the wrong things like: *"I know just how you feel," "it's for the best," "only the good die young," "time heals all wounds," "at least he didn't suffer," "God wanted more flowers in his garden," "keep a stiff upper lip," "you'll be fine."* People may have good intentions when they say these things, but their words are often attempts to stop us from grieving, fix things that can't be fixed, or explain what can't be explained.

Remember that people may try to rush you through your grief. Haugk suggests to seek out people who will really listen to you and who will really accept you (Book 2, p. 38).

The **key** to talking through your grief is finding people who will let you talk and help you heal. Ken says that **H-E-A-L** stands for: <u>H</u>ere for you when you need them, <u>E</u>mpathetic, <u>A</u>ccepting, and <u>L</u>istening. (Book 3, p. 11ff). Theresa Rando in *How to Go on Living When Someone You Love Dies*, says, *"There is no way around the pain that you naturally feel when someone you love dies. You can't go over it, under it, or around it ... Going through it is what will help you heal"* (Book 2, p. 7).

People sometimes are angry at God for what happened. Haugk says, and I agree, that *"it's perfectly okay to be angry with God"* (Book 3, p. 16). The Psalms are filled with many laments as well as expressions of anger (Psalm 22, *"my God, my God, why have your forsaken me ...,"* etc). No matter how hard you beat against God's chest, God's loving arms are waiting to embrace you.

Guilt may also be present. Haugk points out that guilt is only supposed to be a temporary emotion, it is a warning signal for what may need to be corrected. Guilt isn't designed to be permanent. He suggests these ways to let go of guilt: identify and admit your guilt, talk about your guilt, write about your guilt, forgive yourself, pray the serenity prayer, view your guilt as someone else might, remember the good that you did, and embrace the living. Letting go of guilt is another **key** to one's healing.

Book 4, p. 10 ff (see also Book 3, p. 3) has reminders for the second year of grief. Please note that most people will take two to three years to do all the grieving they need to do. Haugk reminds the reader that *"some may take more, and some may take less, because there's no one-size-fits-all time frame for grief."* The reminders are: Continuing upsurges of grief, special days can still be rough, pressure to be 'over it,' pressure to map out the rest of your life, a need to take care of yourself, and continued need for support.

Reflection 6

Are You Worth It?

"So the last will be first, and the first will be last."
— Matthew 20:16

Taxes are a part of life whether we like it or not. April 15th is a day to remember! Sometimes we may wonder about our economic worth after taxes. For those of us who are self-employed we know that our taxes were due on the 15th of September and three other times during the year! In one sense this is what Matthew is all about. He was a tax collector; a despised one no less! And yet, Jesus called him (Matthew 9:9) to be a disciple, a follower of Christ. To Jesus, Matthew was worth more than just a few tax dollars, legally obtained or otherwise!

There are times in our own lives when, we, too, might question the calling of Jesus' followers … or maybe even Jesus' choices. We say to ourselves, there must be standards and rules. There has to be some accountability! For a tax collector, standards, rules, and accountability were all part of the trade.

This parable would present problems for a union boss who had to read these verses before the parish. In fact, that person might even decline to read that Sunday! "Equal pay for unequal work … who are you trying to kid!" Or what about equal pay for both genders! This only leads to raising the minimum wage schedules? Are we not a nation of immigrants? The words on the Statue of Liberty declare: "Give me your tired, hungry and poor"! Some would say, "Equal immigration for all"!?

Yet this is the point … not equality in payment, but equality as demonstrated by God's love and mercy. Not all of us hear God's call at the same time or in the same manner. Some of us take our sweet old time responding to God's call. Others might say, "Where do I sign up?" Regardless of when we come to God, his love and mercy is always waiting for us. All of us receive the same love and mercy from God. You might ask yourself this question: *Is there such a thing as receiving only part of God's love and mercy?*

It seems to me that God is indeed generous. God calls each and every person, from all avenues and walks of life, to serve him with the gift he has given each person. Like Matthew, God calls you. Are you ready? Are you worth it? God's mercy and love endure for ever. Yes, you are worth it, for Christ died for all people, great or small, tax collector or tax avoid-er.

REFLECTION 7

SUMMER SABBATH

And on the seventh day God finished the work that he had done, and he rested on the seventh day from all the work that he had done. So God blessed the seventh day and hallowed it, because on it God rested from all the work that he had done in creation."
- Genesis 2:2-3

Recall that after John the Baptist was beheaded in Mark's Gospel and before the feeding of the five thousand and Jesus walked on the water, the disciples and apostles gathered together and heard Jesus say: "… 'Come away to a deserted place all by yourselves and rest a while.'
— Mark 6:31

The words sound so inviting to rest after a long day at the office, on the road or at the church. It seems like God needed some rest after a day of creating. We all need to rest. We all need to relax. We all need to take time and smell the roses. Taking time is good for the body, mind and spirit. Perhaps Jesus' words need to take hold in our lives. Remember the words to George Gershwin's *Summertime* in *Porgy and Bess*, "Summertime and the living is easy." These words ring true anytime. Think about it: Summer time is a good time to rest and relax … but so is Fall, Winter and Spring!

How often do we need to find some peace and quiet in our lives? Where do we find rest during our stressful lives? The opportunity for some rest and relaxation was provided by the folks at St. Luke's Lutheran Church, Fullerton. Yep, we had a beach day at Huntington Beach … a day to relax and rest!!

In the early morning hours a sweatshirt felt good and a pit fire provided some warmth. Now I ask you to use your imagination … out there somewhere Jesus is walking on the ocean, coming ashore walking towards you, the fire is providing some warmth for the early morning chill. Jesus, the disciples and you … a marvelous image (see Mark 6:45 ff for details of Jesus walking on water; cf. Matthew 14:22-33; John 6:15-21).

After the marine layer burned off, it was a perfect day in the sun. Finding a few sea shells by the rolling sounds of the surf is also calming. Those black sea shells are especially interesting. Watching the sea crabs emerge from their hiding places remind us of being protected. Seeing Catalina Island in the distance is a reminder of terra firma beyond our shores. Of course there was a cool ocean breeze, lots of sun screen, hats with wide brims, and umbrellas to keep the sun away. Besides we all need a little vitamin D provided by the sun.

I heard people saying, "This is just what I needed … some time to sit and relax and enjoy the cool ocean breeze." Read a book, catch up on the latest baseball game. "Hey, how about those Angels, Dodgers, and Cubs?!" Kites were soaring, the volleyballs were whizzing around and an occasional whiffle ball game was in progress. People were walking, running, riding, rollerblading and relaxing.

God gives us opportunities to rest, to recharge our batteries, to be with friends, to learn who we are by taking time to kick back and rest. When we push ourselves too much, we need the space; we need the time to relax and rest.

Both Jesus and Paul remind us to bear one another's burdens (Matthew 11:28-30; Galatians 6:2), to rest and relax. Jesus has come to give us life and to give life more abundantly. Yep, we need to take the time to refresh our body, mind and spirit. Don't forget the sun screen!

Reflection 8

Tears and Death at the US/Mexican Border

At one of our Pacifica Synod Assemblies in San Diego, I was able to participate in a workshop which included a trip on the Red Trolley leaving from the Town & Country Resort to the US/Mexican Border. Seventy-five people traveled with the Salvadoran Lutheran Bishop Medardo Ernesto Gomez to the Tijuana border crossing. Journalists in El Salvador have called Bishop Gomez the "Bishop of the Refugees" because he believes that "God chooses to identify with us, becoming like us ... incarnating God's own self in the people we are" (p. 16, *Fire Against Fire*). Before his election as bishop, Gomez studied theology at the Lutheran Seminary in Mexico City (Seminario Luterano Augsburgo). The journey to the border was an emotional and Spirit-filled experience.

Gomez has served the Lutheran Church of El Salvador as bishop since, 1986. I remember meeting Bishop Gomez at the Lutheran Center in New York City when I was a parish pastor in New Jersey. Bishop Gomez has been nominated for the Nobel Peace Prize. He knew Archbishop Oscar Romero of El Salvador, who was assassinated on March 24, 1980 while saying Mass. Gomez is the author of *Fire Against Fire*, which shares Christian ministry coming face-to-face with persecution. (The book is published by Augsburg, 1989, translated by Mary M. Solberg. Originally published in Spanish, *Fuego contra Fuego*. You may also want to consult, *The Violence of Love: The Pastoral Wisdom of Archbishop Oscar Romero* by Oscar Romero, Translated & compiled by James R. Brockman, S.J., NY: Harper & Row Publishers, 1988).

Bishop Gomez knows first hand about persecution, hatred, and torture. One of his colleagues, Lutheran Pastor David Fernandez of San Miguel, was murdered by soldiers of the Third Brigade. Gomez was persecuted and tortured for the faith during "the violence" in El Salvador.

In several places, stretching for miles, along the California/Mexican border there are actually three separate walls. Nothing prepares a person for the starkness of the border wall. However, the most emotionally charged part of the wall is the hundreds of crosses with names written across them, some adults and others children. Crosses mean death and all along the wall one realizes that one person created in the image of God has died. Just imagine hundreds of crosses ... one on top of the other. The themes of death and resurrection are etched in your psyche.

The seventy-five people in our workshop were visibly moved to tears and openly prayed at the border crossing. I noticed Bishop Gomez bowing his head. He seemed silent for a long long time. We acknowledge that we have problems keeping people out. Yes there are many complaints that jobs are being taken by those who have come here to find work.

The newspapers tell us that there are a variety of drug smugglers, prostitution rings, financial swindlers, abused children and spouses all trying to get in "to the promised land." A border guard said that "... thousands of people cross the border each day with the hopes of beginning a new life."

After leaving the border we walked to the Border Community Center to hear stories from fellow pastors about their experiences of crossing the border. Bishop Gomez confessed that he "was moved to pray" and that "tears came to his eyes." He shared his understanding of a "theology of life" lived out by the people of El Salvador. Another pastor shared her border crossing story as a teenager (age 19) with a child and being separated from her child for several days. What a powerful experience ... this workshop at the border crossing. "In Christ there is no east or west, north or south, no Jew or Gentile, no male or female, we are all one in Christ ..." (Galatians 3:28-29, Luke 13:29-30). In Christ there are no borders, in fact Jesus always seems to be reaching out to those who are on the fringes of society. After all, what is a border to God, to Jesus, or to the Holy Spirit?

(Resource: Lutheran Border Concerns Ministry (LBCM), 3060 54th Street, San Diego, CA 92105-4924, 619-286-2445 or www.lutherborderconcernsministry.org. NOTE: LBCM is a non-profit independent, inter-Lutheran organization incorporated in California since 1967.)

REFLECTION 9

WHERE ANGELS FEAR TO TREAD

"In that region there were shepherds living in the fields, keeping watch over their flock by night. Then an angel of the Lord stood before them, and the glory of the Lord shone around them, and they were terrified. But the angel said to them, "Do not be afraid; for see—I am bringing you good news of great joy for all the people: ..."

– Luke 2:9-10*

Part of my role as chaplain (CHP) with Trinity Care Hospice (TCH) is to provide spiritual care to individuals and families who are open to the presence of a spiritual care provider. Hospice professionals (physicians [MDs], nurses [RNs], social workers [MSWs], and chaplains [CHPs]) visit people in their homes, nursing homes (skilled nursing facilities [SNFs]), board & care facilities (B & C), and even hospitals.

Several weeks ago I was asked by my Torrance Patient Care Manager (PCM, RN) to visit a recently admitted hospice patient, Maria, who was close to death and at Little Company of Mary Hospital (LCMH), Torrance. The goal was for Maria to return to her own home. I already knew that Maria had a Roman Catholic background. As requested by the family, the MSW arranged for a priest from the hospital to visit the patient over the weekend. The patient, along with the family, requested the sacrament of "the anointing of the sick." The priest from LCMH visited Maria, shared "the anointing of the sick" and the family was comforted. It was reported that Maria did not verbally respond during the priest's visit.

The day that I visited Maria – she was unresponsive and unable to talk because of the disease process (and Maria only speaks Spanish, being originally from Bolivia). Maria was also using oxygen. The oldest daughter, Lupe, was in the room when I arrived. I introduced myself and Lupe shared that her mother had been unresponsive, unable to talk, but appeared comfortable and in no pain. I was aware of Maria's irregular breathing and shared this with Lupe. Lupe had already read *Gone From My Sight* (in Spanish, *Desaparecio de mi Vista*), a pamphlet shared with families by TCH, and was aware of her mother's irregular breathing. She thanked me for coming so promptly. Lupe was very thankful for the hospice team and couldn't say enough about the care her mother was receiving. I asked if she wanted me to pray and read Scripture with her. Lupe said "yes." I read several selections from the psalms. During the prayer, Lupe also offered her petitions. In addition, I was aware of emotions beginning to surface in me. Some deeper connection had been made with the daughter and mother after only ten minutes. When I finished the prayer, Lupe said, "I know my mother is in good hands and you hospice workers are angels." When Lupe said that, I began to cry. What really made the tears flow was when Lupe offered me some tissues. I thanked her and she said again, "You are angels … all of you." Maria seemed comfortable and Lupe was smiling. I learned later in the day that Maria had died shortly after I left the room. It was a peaceful death and Lupe was thankful that I was there to pray and offer my presence.

It was an emotional visit and stirred my humanity and compassion for this family. During bereavement support the next day, I shared this visit with my colleagues, saying that I was touched by this family and that I was deeply moved by the Spirit to share my humanity and cry in their presence. I was supported and affirmed. Hospice touches many individuals and families with compassion, love, and understanding.

*Read the whole story about the birth of Jesus in Luke 2:1-20.

REFLECTION 10

HUMOR? OH YES!

Norman Cousins has written a classic, *Anatomy of an Illness*. Hospital and hospice chaplains, parish pastors, ministers, rabbis, imams as well as a host of spiritual guides will find this book of interest because it highlights Cousins healthcare journey in combating a life threatening illness (ankylosing spondylitis, severe connective tissue [collagen] disease … which means that the connective tissue in the spine was disintegrating, pp. 32-33) by using humor and participating in his care. By the way, all arthritic and rheumatic diseases are in this category … collagen disease.

Endorphins are important! What about your endorphins, how are they doing?

Though not a healthcare professional, his positive influence on the healing arts of our era has been immense. *Anatomy of an Illness* started the revolution in patients working with their physicians and using humor to boost their bodies' capacity for healing.

After returning from a grueling trip to the Soviet Union in 1964, Cousins was admitted to a hospital with a very high sedimentation rate (88 rising to 115. NOTE: sedimentation rate measures the degree of inflammation or infection, p. 30). His physician, Dr. William Hitzig, informed him that his chances of recovery were around 1 in 500, prompting him to 'get in on the act' (pp. 33 and 41).

Cousins perceptively concluded early on that his hospital regimen of lifeless food, powerful anti-inflammatory medications and constant interruptions was a recipe for disaster. In response, he did something quite radical for the time – he used his layperson's intellect to explore the nature of his disease, and to fashion an unconventional protocol for recovery. The self-confidence born of his leadership position in America's intellectual community (he was editor of the influential *Saturday Review*) served him extremely well.

Concluding that he would not recover if he continued with the suppressive medications that were (and still are) the medical standard of care for such diseases, yet understanding the need to counteract the debilitating effects of the inflammatory process at work in his body, Cousins forged ahead with a regimen built on megadoses of both Vitamin C and laughter. He combined the vitamin doses with a steady diet of "Candid Camera" and the Marx Brothers (p. 43). He found that "ten minutes of genuine belly laughter had an anesthetic effect and would give him at least two hours of pain-free sleep" (p. 43).

In the chapter on Creativity and Longevity (Chapter 3, p. 79ff), Cousins focuses on Pablo Casals and Albert Schweitzer. He met them both when they were in their eighties. Both were musicians, and both were devoted to Bach, playing his music every day. Music was their medicine but also their humor.

Cousins recalls an amusing incident where Dr. Albert Schweitzer reported that "as everyone knows, there are only two automobiles within seventy-five miles of the hospital. This afternoon the inevitable happened: they collided. We have treated the drivers for their superficial wounds. Anyone who has reverence for machines may treat the cars" (p. 92). Can you hear the laughter??!!

Cousins was blessed with a physician "who knew that his biggest job was to encourage the patient's will to live and to mobilize all the natural resources of the body and mind to combat disease" (p. 49).

Though he waited more than a decade after his recovery before telling his story to a wide audience, his landmark 1976 article in the *New England Journal of Medicine* (actually Chapter 1, pages 29-54 of *Anatomy of an Illness*) opened the floodgates (see Chapter 1 & 6, "What I Learned from Three Thousand Doctors," p. 139ff). Thousands of physicians and patients responded with a groundswell of interest in mind-body medicine that continues to this day.

In fact, the model of mind-body-spirit has been reflected by a holistic team approach, including physicians, nurses, social workers, and chaplains in hospitals, hospices and in general throughout healthcare systems. The mind-body-spirit model is now considered part of the 'best practice' modality in healthcare as well as congregational settings. We are more than just our bodies. Our mind and spirit are just as important!

It goes without saying that we are more than a mind, more than a body and yes even more than a spirit. St. Paul says that we are part of one another. For example, the foot cannot say it doesn't need the hand (Romans 12; 1 Corinthians 12:12 ff) the hand cannot say it doesn't need the eye ... as Paul says, "for in fact the body is not one member but many" (1 Corinthians 12:14). We are connected.

In the final years of his life (he died at age 75 on November 30, 1990 in Los Angeles), he employed his considerable talents in affiliation with the UCLA School of Medicine, working to instill a truly holistic (see Chapter 5, "Holistic Health and Healing," 121 ff) and compassionate perspective in a profession whose conventional methods too often blind it to simple but profound truths.

Anatomy of an Illness was first published in 1979, with an anniversary edition in 2005. Computers, tablets, smart phones, smart televisions, iPhones, iPads, iPods, iReaders, Nooks, Kindles, etc have all changed the way we communicate since 1979. Technology continues to evolve. Now you can view a YouTube interview (ten minutes) with Cousins discussing *Anatomy of an Illness* and his early hospitalization of over a year with TB as a young child.

In addition, Cousins was portrayed by actor Ed Asner in a 1984 television movie, *Anatomy of an Illness*, which was based on Cousins' 1979 book, *Anatomy of an Illness as Perceived by the Patient*.

By reflecting on the mind-body-spirit modality, Cousins provides excellent resources in an extended bibliography (180-192). Cousins has also published, *Head First: The Biology of Hope and the Healing Power of the Human Spirit*; *Human Options: An Autobiographical Notebook*; *The Pathology of Power*, discusses the rise of the military industrial complex; and *Easy Cycling Around Vancouver* with his wife Jean Cousins.

Finally, don't forget that humor is important and may even lead to a few breakthroughs. By the way, ever since I've been a hospice chaplain family and friends have referred to me as "Charley Chaplain!" I hear you laughing!!!

REFLECTION 11

THE MOURNER'S CODE

For 'In him we live and move and have our being'; as even some of your own poets have said, 'For we too are his offspring.'
— Acts 17:28

Jesus Christ is the same yesterday and today and forever.

— Hebrews 13:8

Alan Wolfelt is a grief educator. He has written many helpful resources for grieving people. The best place to contact Dr. Wolfelt is through his website: www.centerforloss.com. You may also write or call: The Center for Loss and Life Transition, 3735 Broken Bow Road, Fort Collins, Colorado 80526, 970-226-6050.

In the second edition of *The Journey Through Grief: Reflections On Healing*, Wolfelt shares his Mourner's Code. He writes: "the following list is intended both to empower you to heal and to decide how others can and cannot help. This is not to discourage you from reaching out to others for help, but rather to assist you in distinguishing useful responses from hurtful ones." (p. 161)

1. You have the right to experience your own unique grief. No one else will grieve in exactly the same way you do. So, when you turn to others for help, don't allow them to tell you what you should or should not be feeling.

2. You have the right to talk about your grief. Talking about your grief will help you heal. Seek out others who will allow you to talk as much as you want, as often as you want, about your grief. If at times you don't feel like talking, you also have the right to be silent.

3. You have the right to feel a multitude of emotions. Confusion, numbness, disorientation, fear, guilt and relief are just a few of the emotions you might feel as part of your grief journey.

4. You have the right to be tolerant of your physical and emotional limits. Your feelings of loss and sadness will probably leave you feeling fatigued. Respect what your body and mind are telling you. Get daily rest. Eat balanced meals.

5. You have the right to experience "griefbursts." Sometimes, out of nowhere, a powerful surge of grief may overcome you. This can be frightening, but it is normal and natural. Find someone who understands and will let you talk it out.

6. You have the right to make use of ritual. The funeral ritual does more than acknowledge the death of someone loved. It helps provide you with the support of caring people.

7. You have the right to embrace your spirituality. If faith is a part of your life, express it in ways that seem appropriate to you. Allow yourself to be around people who understand and support your religious beliefs. If you feel angry at God, find someone to talk with who won't be critical of your feelings of hurt and abandonment.

8. You have the right to search for meaning. You may find yourself asking, "why did he or she die? Why this way? Why now? Some of your questions may have answers, but some may not.

9. You have the right to treasure your memories. Memories are one of the best legacies that exist after the death of someone loved. You will always remember. Instead of ignoring your memories, find others with whom you can share them.

10. You have the right to move toward your grief and heal. Reconciling your grief will not happen quickly. Remember, grief is a process, not an event. Be patient and tolerant with yourself and avoid people who are impatient with and intolerant of you. Neither you nor those around you must forget that the death of someone loved changes your life forever.

Dr. Wolfelt reminds us that "in some ways, love and grief are very much alike. They both have the power to forever change our lives. Just as I must surrender to love, I must surrender to my grief."

REFLECTION 12

THE BRONZE BOOT

There is no longer Jew or Greek, there is no longer slave or free, there is no longer male and female; for all of you are one in Christ Jesus.

– Galatians 3:28

More readings: Leviticus 19:18, Matthew 22:34-40, Mark 12:28-31, Luke 10:25-28

I will always remember the "bronze boot." Physicians, nurses, social workers, chaplains, and home health aids are at one time or another affected by the people they visit. Some people make lasting impressions. From a chaplain's perspective, Harry made an impression on me. I will always think of forgiveness and the bronze boot when I think of Harry.

Harry received the bronze boot for his many years of service with the United States Army. He proudly displayed the bronze boot and other military honors in the room where he eventually died. Anyone who visited heard about the bronze boot. Harry loved this country and served the United States of America with dignity, pride and honor.

Whenever I visited, Harry remembered his military time in Italy during World War II. Harry was wounded and spent some time recovering in a military hospital in Europe. Tears came to Harry's eyes as he shared a story about asking for a chaplain. One day a chaplain was making rounds and stopped near Harry's bed. What Harry shared next was hard to imagine during war time.

Harry requested that the chaplain pray with him and he asked for his favorite psalm to be read – Psalm 23. The chaplain responded by saying that Harry needed to ask for "his own kind of chaplain." You see, Harry, was African American and the chaplain was white. It seems as though the military still had segregated troops during World War II. Tears came to Harry's eyes even now as I listened to his story. What Harry said next was even more amazing and revealing of Harry's character, "You know I forgave that chaplain for saying those hurtful words." I started to cry and thanked Harry for sharing. Harry had touched me with words of gentleness and forgiveness.

Harry asked me to be at his memorial service. I remember sharing these words with the family at Inglewood Cemetery, "…love the Lord your God with all your heart, and with all your soul, and with all your strength, and with all your mind; and love your neighbor as yourself." Harry not only loved God, Harry loved his neighbors as well.

Harry's children - Mildred who works for the city of Los Angeles, and two sons, Ricky and Tony, are both captains with the Los Angeles Fire Department, loved their father (mother died thirteen years ago) and recognized the strength he shared with them to live in this world filled with people of color, diversity and prejudice. Thanks be to God for Harry and all people of this world who practice forgiveness.

Reflection 13

Remembrance and Transformation: An Evening with Thich Nhat Hanh

Thich Nhat Hanh, is a Buddhist monk I will long remember. I heard Thich Nhat Hanh and the monks from the Deer Park Monastery, Escondido, CA, (www.deerparkmonastery.org) on two separate occasions at the Pasadena Civic Auditorium, Pasadena, California.

On both occasions we were led by the monks in the practice of mindfulness, with an emphasis on the awareness of our breath, that is "breathing in and breathing out," and reflecting on peaceful words. I was reminded to "breathe, you are alive!"

I experienced the peacefulness of being present with myself, allowing myself to relax and listen to my body. The soothing chants, ringing of the large bowl, and the singing of the monks (women on one side; men on the other) was both calming and soothing. Several poems about Vietnam, one written over 40 years ago by Hanh, brought tears to my eyes. Hanh was seen as a threat in his home country, Vietnam. He was banned from teaching there for many years.

Practicing mindfulness includes the four truths:

1. Suffering is present.
2. Asking questions.
3. Compassionate listening.
4. Practicing loving speech.

Hanh gave examples of practicing loving speech: in marriage relationships, with the survivors of Hurricane Katrina, the Gulf War, 9/11, Israelis and Palestinians, and the healing of our own country. Peacefulness and compassionate listening are needed in all examples.

Thich Nhat Hanh was nominated for the Nobel Peace Prize by the Rev. Martin Luther King, Jr in 1967. He said, "When we are mindful, deeply in touch with the present moment, our understanding of what is going on deepens, and we begin to be filled with acceptance, joy, peace and love."

Hanh has lived half of his 80 years in Vietnam and the other half in the USA. Christians and Buddhists need to continue the dialogue.

Helpful Resources by Thich Nhat Hanh include: *Living Buddha, Living Christ*, (NY: Riverhead Books, 1995); *The Miracle of Mindfulness: A Manual on Meditation*, (Boston: Beacon Press, 1975, 1976); *The Heart of the Buddha's Teaching*, (NY: Broadway Books, 1998, 1999). *Transformation and Healing: The Sutra on the Four Establishments of Mindfulness*, (Berkeley, CA: Parallax Press, 1990); *No Death, No Fear: Comforting Wisdom for Life*, (NY: Riverhead Books, 2002); and *Touching Peace: Practicing the Art of Mindful Living*, (Berkeley, CA: Parallax Press, 1992).

A Morning and Afternoon with the Dalai Lama

Another memorable experience was held at San Diego State University. There wasn't an empty seat in the house!! The space where the San Diego State University basketball team plays couldn't have been more stimulating. One could almost see Steve Fisher (Illinois State '67), Head Coach of the SDSU Aztecs, going through some exercises with the team!! It was a three-day symposium for the Dalai Lama in San Diego. The Dalai Lama visited and held lectures at three San Diego universities: SDSU; University of California, San Diego; and the University of San Diego.

"Compassion Without Borders: Science, Peace, Ethics" was the timely topic. The arrival of the Dalai Lama was tremendous! Tenzin Gyatso is the 14th and current Dalai Lama. A Tibetan Buddhist and Nobel Peace Prize recipient in 1989 led the filled auditorium with stories, humor, and challenges. He wore the San

Diego State University baseball cap throughout his reflections!! The Dalai Lama emphasized self-discipline as a working principle for all cultures. I still recall this phrase from him: "Compassion seems to be the greatest power."

Resources by the Dalai Lama: *In My Own Words. An Introduction to My Teachings and Philosophy*, Rajiv Mehrotra, ed. (New York City: Hay House, Inc, 2008); *My Spiritual Journey: Personal Reflections, Teachings, and Talks,* Collection by Sofia Stril-Rever, (Harper One, 2011); *Beyond Religion: Ethics for a Whole World*, (Boston: Houghton Mifflin Harcourt, 2011); and *Toward A True Kinship of Faiths: How the World's Religions Can Come Together*, (NY: Three Rivers Press, 2010).

Reflection 14

Spiritual Presence During Parathyroid Surgery

Have you ever felt the spiritual presence of God in your life? What about the presence of God during surgery? I have felt God's presence many times in my life, usually at times when I least expected God (see 1 Kings 19:12; Isaiah 40:31; Psalm 46:10). I sensed that the *'still small voice of God'*, God's presence, was with me during my recent surgery.

On a routine physical, which I do every other year, the blood lab results showed that I had a high calcium level (10.2 is the top level). My calcium level was 10.3. My internist, Dr. Martha Sosa Johnson, UC Irvine, wanted to check this out to see if there was anything to the elevated calcium. High calcium levels can potentially lead to a host of serious issues, including osteoporosis.

My journey to discover the cause of the high calcium level included the following tests: bone density scan, followed by several more blood tests and a sonogram on my parathyroid (throat area).

The results showed an adenoma on the right posterior parathyroid, about the size of a small cucumber seed. The parathyroid gland, according to **Mosby's Medical Dictionary,** is *"any one of several small structures, usually four, attached to the dorsal surfaces of the lateral lobes of the thyroid gland. The parathyroid glands secrete parathyroid hormone, which helps maintain the blood calcium concentration and ensures normal neuromuscular irritability, blood clotting, and cell membrane permeability"* (p. 1398-1399, Mosby's).

Regarding my lab results, I quote UC, Irvine physician Bogi Andersen, MD, on 12/02/08, "these findings are consistent with parathyroid adenoma in the posterior aspect of the right inferior hemithyroid." I was referred to Dr. John Butler, at the Chao Family Cancer Center, Chief of Surgical Oncology at UC, Irvine. After my consultation with Dr. Butler, (02/04/09), surgery was recommended. There was no rush for the surgery. Needless to say, I was a little anxious. Not knowing what was ahead can cause some sleepless nights and I don't live in Seattle (movie reference to *Sleepless in Seattle*).

My previous surgery was at age seventeen at the Billings Memorial Hospital on the campus of the University of Chicago. That surgery was a local anesthetic. This surgery would require more. Do you sense my anxiety rising?

If the anxiety was not high enough, my wife, Nancy, was recovering from bunion and hammer toe surgery on both of her feet (early January 2009). She was off work for four months. During her recovery, she learned to use the wheelchair and walker around home. She also had several follow-up visits with her podiatrist surgeon as well as months of physical therapy.

My surgery was scheduled for Friday, July 31st. On the first pre-op meeting with Dr. Butler, I learned that he had a Roman Catholic background and was active in his local Roman Catholic parish attending and leading Bible studies. I shared with Dr. Butler that I was a Lutheran pastor and hospice chaplain and wanted to be able to sing the liturgy again. He fully understood! Several days before the surgery, I had an EKG, chest x-ray, and more blood work.

On the day of the surgery, I handed Dr. Butler a summary of my medications (which he already knew) along with an indication that the surgery was for the **right parathyroid**. He marked the right side of my throat in bright blue! I also shared with Dr. Butler that I had been praying for him and the operating team.

Since this was my first anesthetic, I was anxious and didn't know what to expect. I wanted to wake up again and sing praises to God. Dr. Butler shared with me that *he had been praying for me.* When he said this I said, *"Thank you!"* He also shared that he prays for **all** his patients. I was touched by his compassion and prayer. Do you sense the presence of God?

Furthermore, on the day of the surgery, I recall being in the prep room where an anxious RN could not find a vein to insert the needle. After several tries on the left hand, the anxious RN inserted the needle into my right hand. While in the prep room, I met the anesthesiologist, the operating room RN, and Dr. Butler.

I recall the short ride from the prep room to the operating room. The operating room was well lighted, I noticed lots of equipment. The nurse in the operating room asked if I could go from the gurney to the operating table. She asked me to be sure to position myself onto the center of the operating table, I recall that the table was quite narrow. I asked her, *"Is this okay ... am I centered?"* That's the last I remember until I was in the recovery room, two hours later, where my wife was asking me how I felt! She said, "You kept saying, *'m...hm, m...hm, u...hm....'" 'yes...'"*

Throughout the operation I had the sense of being held in the loving hands of Jesus. I felt surrounded by the love of God. I wondered if the angels were present? My sense is that the angels were present!

The image of an **old Russian icon** that of the Madonna with Child came to mind after the surgery. The icon depicts the mother of Jesus holding Jesus, cradling him, protecting him in her loving arms. It is a safe image and a safe feeling. God's love surrounds people whether they know it or not.

Upon further reflection, I recall that my own mother died suddenly this past March (3/16/2009). She, too, had held me in her arms when I was a baby. She had cradled me in her loving arms. All these connections of prayer, being held by the love of God, being held by my own mother, and even a sense of being surrounded by angels flooded my memory. God is good and God is love (1 John 4:8) and God loves us. God is the Creator and we are the creations of God's love. There was a sense of God's presence in my room and throughout this surgery experience.

Many verses from the Psalms remind us of God's presence. *"Be still and know that I am God"* (Psalm 46:10). Psalm 136 says: *"Oh, give thanks to the LORD, for He is good! For His mercy endures forever"* (Psalm 136:1ff). Again the Psalmist says: *"... the LORD is good; His mercy is everlasting, and his truth endures to all generations"* (Psalm 100:5).

St. Paul tells us that God has given us *"every spiritual blessing …"* (Ephesians 1:3) and so we give thanks to God for all the spiritual blessings we have received. Let us have the passion to give thanks to God for life *"for whether we live or whether we die, we are the Lord's"* (Romans 14:7).

OVERNIGHT AT THE HOSPITAL

Another lesson learned was that staying in the hospital overnight is not the place to find rest! Perhaps you already know this little gem.

Some of what happens to an individual relates to post-surgery care for the kind of surgery the individual has experienced. No two surgeries are the same, hence after care is vital. It seemed to me that every four hours my vital signs were taken, including blood pressure, oxygen level, temperature (using a head thermometer), and respirations. Medications were given every six hours or as needed for pain. Fortunately I had no pain.

Just when I would drift off, the RN would show up asking for my blood pressure, more medications, or the ever present urinal. I noticed that my output of fluids was about 300 milliliters every two hours. So every two, four, and six hours there were interruptions. No rest. Besides there were no baseball games on television, just ESPN with sports updates. I thought to myself, *"two, four, six, eight, who do we appreciate, let's go home and hibernate!"* I needed some rest!

After the surgery I did at least fifteen laps around the nursing station. I wanted to show the nurses that I was ready to go home. The following morning, after breakfast, I did at least twenty-five laps around the nurses' station. Around noon, the word came … you have been discharged! Of course, this was preceded by the surgeon coming to see how the patient was doing. The healing continues and God's presence is all around.

Since I stayed overnight, I did re-read William A. Barry's book, *Letting God Come Close* (Loyola Press, Chicago, 2001). Barry's words made an impact on me, *"... God can be found in all things ...every human experience has a religious dimension and religious meaning."* (p.91) God is present and God was present in my surgery. Let us rejoice and give thanks!

REFLECTION 15

IT'S WHAT'S INSIDE THAT COUNTS!

BUDDHISTS, CHRISTIANS, HINDUS, JEWS, AND MUSLIMS

> *Hear, O Israel: The Lord is our God, the Lord alone.*
> —Deuteronomy 6:4

> *Owe no one anything, except to love one another; for the one who loves another has fulfilled the law. The commandments, "You shall not commit adultery; You shall not murder; You shall not steal; You shall not covet"; and any other commandment, are summed up in this word, "Love your neighbor as yourself." Love does no wrong to a neighbor; therefore, love is the fulfilling of the law.*
> — Romans 13:8-10

As a hospice chaplain, I have visited many people who express a variety of religious traditions and practices as Buddhists, Hindus, Mormons, Jews, Muslims and of course, Christians, be they evangelicals, protestants, Roman Catholics, or Orthodox. Hospice ministry is an enriching religious experience. Regardless of a person's religious background or experience, I have found that it's *what's inside a person* that is spiritually revealing.

Thomas Merton once wrote:

> Our real journey in life is interior. It is a matter of growth, deepening, and of an ever greater surrender to the creative action of love and grace in our hearts.

As a hospice spiritual care provider, we encounter individuals and families who are on various religious and spiritual paths. Providing **love and presence** when someone is dying is the bridge that touches the spiritual being. Merton is right, the "real journey in life is interior," and **it is what's inside a person that really counts**. Even the atheist and agnostic seem to warm up to the **love and presence** of a hospice spiritual care provider. Human life is sacred. Hence, the dimension of the holy can indeed be a mystery.

When Jesus was asked which commandment was the most important, he quoted Deuteronomy and perhaps looked inside people when he said, " … love the LORD your God with all your heart, and with all your soul, and with all your might ..." to which the New Testament adds, "... and love your neighbor as yourself." (Deuteronomy 6:4-6, Mark 122:29-30, Matthew 22:34-40, Luke 10:25-28) The words from Deuteronomy in the Hebrew Scriptures are known as the *Shema,* meaning, "hear." Loving God and loving your neighbor seem obvious. **Practicing love and presence** also make a tremendous difference in a person's life.

As I visit people with various religious backgrounds, I find myself repeating Merton's prayer:

> My Lord God, I have no idea where I am going. I do not see the road ahead of me. I cannot know for certain where it will end. Nor do I really know myself and the fact that I think I am following your will does not mean that I am actually doing so. But I believe that the desire to please you does in fact please you. And I hope I have that desire in all that I am doing. I ope that I will never do anything apart from that desire. And I know that if I do this you will lead me by the right road, though I may know nothing about it. Therefore I will trust you always though I may seem to be lost and in the shadow of death. I will not fear, for you are ever with me, and you will never leave me to face my perils alone.
>
> – from *Thoughts in Solitude.* 1958

To expand my understanding of religious traditions, I have found two resources by Huston Smith, who most recently was visiting professor at the University of California, Berkeley helpful. *The World's Religions* (revised and updated edition, 1991, originally published in 1958 with the title *The Religions of Man*) and *Why Religion Matters: The Fate of the Human Spirit in an Age of Disbelief,* 2001. Indeed, the ancient mystics reflected, " ... we must allow the presence of God to shine forth."

REFLECTION 16

A SILENT RETREAT AND THE MISSING THUMB

Several years ago I made a silent directed retreat at the Center for Spiritual Development, Orange, California. The Center is near both St. Joseph & Children's Hospitals.

While on retreat, I enjoyed walking around the campus after meals. There are many statues and solitary places with benches for contemplation. One particular concrete statue was a standing Mary holding baby Jesus. Somehow the baby Jesus was missing his left thumb. How odd, I thought.

Recently I attended a seminar at the Center. After lunch I took a walk. The abundant flowers and landscaping is impressive. The vibrant flower colors were a delight to the eyes, bright reds, deep purples and a large area with yellow and orange succulents. The statue of the standing Mary holding baby Jesus was nearby. I was surprised to see that the baby Jesus now had a left thumb … it wasn't missing this time! In fact, a white rose was tucked under the left thumb and it appeared as if the baby Jesus was presenting the rose to the on-looker.

Not long ago we celebrated the Resurrection of Our Lord. It is Spring and the smell of jasmine bushes fills the air. Off in the distance stand several large jacaranda trees with their purple flowers as well as several large palm trees. What a glorious sight … lots of color, plants, trees, and lots of places to contemplate.

If you are ever in Orange near St. Joseph and Children's Hospitals, stop by the Center for Spiritual Development, locate the standing Mary holding the baby Jesus. See if his left thumb is still there and if he is holding another rose for you. God bless your contemplative time.

REFLECTION 17

HAVE YOU SEEN THE LIGHT?

Again Jesus spoke to them, saying, "I am the light of the world. Whoever follows me will never walk in darkness but will have the light of life."

– John 8:12

More Readings: Matthew 2:1-12, Ephesians 3:1-12

For some people the word "chaplain" can cause fear, trembling and anxiety. Chaplains provide spiritual care, asking a person what their goal is for the next several days or even hours. Chaplains do more listening and reflecting than prescribing a particular religious path to follow. Catherine did not want to talk with the chaplain. In order to complete the hospice spiritual assessment I had a conversation with Catherine's niece, Gayle. Gayle shared, "Catherine has no religious background. She does not attend church. However she may want to see you in the future." Somehow I felt the door had been left open for a visit.

Catherine had a peaceful death the other day. Along with the social worker I was called to be with the family in their time of grief, shock and sorrow. Gayle shared some wonderful images while visiting with her Aunt Catherine.

One of those images occurred in Gayle's room shortly before she went to visit her Aunt for the last time. Gayle said that there was a tremendous rush of air in her room; the drapes went flying, and she could feel the air all around her. It was a comforting feeling. Gayle felt surrounded by the presence of love. Gayle thought to herself, "this must be the angels coming for my Aunt."

Gayle also recalled a time when Catherine shared that she was in a spacious dark room. Catherine could only see a tiny sliver of light coming from a partially open door. As Catherine approached the door, she heard a little boy say, "you can't come in yet." Catherine tried to push the door open but the little boy kept holding the door shut. It wasn't until our conversation that Gayle remembered that Catherine's youngest brother had died when he was seven years old.

Perhaps that vision and light was from the next dimension where Catherine's brother was waiting. It wasn't Catherine's time yet. Now the door has been opened and what lies beyond this world has been opened to Catherine. Have you seen the light?

Sometimes medical personnel say that visions like this may be the result of lack of oxygen. This may well be the case. Lack of oxygen may produce some interesting hallucinations and visions. Even though we need oxygen to survive in this world, we may not need oxygen in the next dimension.

Two important resources for your own research into the light: Raymond Moody, MD, in *Life After Life*, has written a classic on near death experiences. And Elisabeth Kübler-Ross, MD also shares her experiences in *The Tunnel and the Light*. May the light be with you!

REFLECTION 18

WILL THE REAL CHARLEY CHAPLAIN PLEASE STAND UP!

(NO, THIS ISN'T MISSPELLED!)

"Master, now you are dismissing your servant[e]in peace, according to your word; for my eyes have seen your salvation, which you have prepared in the presence of all peoples, a light for revelation to the Gentiles and for glory to your people Israel."
– Luke 2:29-32

Resources like *Patch Adams*, the book and the movie, (and *Gesundheit! Bringing Good Health to You, the Medical System, and Society through Physician Service, Complementary Therapies, Humor, and Joy*, by Patch Adams, MD with Maureen Mylander, Rochester, VT: Healing Arts Press, 1993, 1998); Bernie Siegel, MD's material in *Love, Medicine & Miracles* (published in 1986 and *Peace, Love and Healing*, 1989); also work by Larry Dosey and others have touched the lives of patients for many years.

Siegal wrote, "unconditional love is the most powerful stimulant of the immune system. The truth is: love heals. Miracles happen to exceptional patients every day – patients who have the courage to love, those who have the courage to work with their doctors to participate in and influence their own recovery."

Recently a chaplain of a different sort got into the act, so to speak. It is historical knowledge that Charley Chaplin would spend summers in Hermosa Beach at 32 Tenth Street, just a stone's throw away from the Pacific Ocean. Just imagine the parties!

Reflection 19

The River is Wide and the Water is Cold or A River Gathering

In those days Jesus came from Nazareth of Galilee and was baptized by John in the Jordan. And just as he was coming up out of the water, he saw the heavens torn apart and the Spirit descending like a dove on him. And a voice came from heaven, "You are my Son, the Beloved; with you I am well pleased."

— Mark 1:9-11

Robert Lowry, pastor at Hanson Place Baptist Church in Brooklyn, New York (1861-1869), wrote the words to *Shall We Gather at the River* in 1864. What the hymn doesn't tell us is that an epidemic was claiming many lives in New York City. It was a frightening time. People were asking each other, "Will we meet again?"

The first verse invites us to gather at the river: "Shall we gather at the river, where bright angel feet have trod, with its crystal tide forever flowing by the throne of God?" Then the refrain washes over us: "Yes, we'll gather at the river, the beautiful, the beautiful river, Gather with the saints at the river that flows by the throne of God."

Maybe you have been to a river, any river for that matter, like the Colorado, the Mississippi, or just a little old river near your home town. Rivers still transport goods and services. I remember the GREEN Chicago River. The river was not green all the time and it was not green from pollution but it could have been. The Chicago River was green from green dye added by the edict of Mayor Richard J. Daly for every St. Patrick's Day Celebration, which included the parade down Michigan Avenue.

Imagine what happens when we reach the river ... the fourth verse says, "Soon we'll reach the shining river, soon our pilgrimage will cease; soon our happy hearts will quiver with the melody of peace." And then the lovely refrain: "Yes, we'll gather at the river, the beautiful, the beautiful river, Gather with the saints at the river that flows by the throne of God."

Legend has it that baby Moses was put in a basket and floated down the Nile River and ultimately was pulled out of the river by one of Pharaoh's servants. Rivers and water are important in the biblical record. Jesus spent some time around the Jordan River and did many lake crossings on the Sea of Galilee. We need water to survive and our internal organs thrive on water lubrication.

So the next time you go to the river, think about the words *Shall We Gather at the River*. One day, we too, will cross over the river, gathered with the saints, in peace and happiness, in that river that flows by the throne of God.

Reflection 20

Greek Orthodox Church

Beloved, let us love one another, because love is from God; everyone who loves is born of God and knows God. Whoever does not love does not know God, for God is love.

– 1 John 4:7-8

Read more: the whole of 1 John 4

The Evangelical Lutheran Church in America (ELCA) and the Orthodox Church have had dialogues for many years (www.elca.org/ecumenical). One day my wife and I attended the Divine Liturgy at Saint John the Baptist Greek Orthodox Church, Anaheim (www.stjohnanaheim.org). We planned to attend worship first and then follow up with the Greek Festival after the liturgy. By the way, Greek foods are great!

We always enjoy the liturgy and the icons. Whenever one worships in an orthodox church one feels surrounded by the saints. The eyes of the saints seem to be looking at you … watching to see what you are doing and what is happening in the world. The dome of the church had a painting of Christ Pantocrator, that is, the all-ruling Christ, representing Christ looking down through heaven upon the assembled congregation, reminding them of Christ's all-pervading presence in the universe.

Part of the service was in Greek and, lucky for me, I still remember my Greek from college and seminary days. *Kyrie Eleison*, or "Lord have mercy" was the response to the prayer petitions. Lutherans continue to use the *Kyrie* in worship. The priest shared a homily based on the story from Luke 24:13-35, the Emmaus walk when Jesus was revealed to the men "in the breaking of the bread." Interesting that Scripture says that the men said: "did not our heart burn within us while He talked with us on the road, and while He opened the Scriptures to us?" One is captivated by the awe and mystery in orthodoxy ... and perhaps our hearts burned while we were there worshiping at Saint John the Baptist. We know that even though we are separated as Eastern & Western Christians we still remain brothers and sisters in the faith. We both claim the name of Christ for our faith, hope and salvation.

At one point in the St. John Chrysostom (349-407 CE, the "golden- mouthed" preacher, as he came to be called) liturgy in both Greek and English, the priest said, "Christ is in our midst." To which we responded, "He is and will ever be."

When Holy Communion was celebrated we ended up being the last ones in line. As my wife approached, the priest said, "Are you Orthodox Christian?" She said, "I'm a Christian ..." We may be one in Christ but not at this altar and not in this Orthodox Church. Nevertheless, it was good liturgy and the icons made the worship special ... we were "surrounded by a great cloud of witnesses" (Hebrews 12:1). Let us continue to pray for the unity of Christ's church (John 17) among the Eastern and Western Christians. We also remembered in our prayers, Archbishop Iakovos, head of the Orthodox Church of North & South America, who had recently died.

Resources/Pamphlets: "Welcome to the Orthodox Liturgy, A Personal Welcome to the Orthodox Church, and The Eastern Orthodox Church: Who Are We?" – St. John's Weekly Bulletin.

The Orthodox Church by Timothy Ware. (Baltimore, Maryland: Penguin Books, 1963).

Orthodox Spirituality: An Outline of the Orthodox Ascetical and Mystical Tradition, by A Monk of the Eastern Church, Third Edition, (Crestwood, NY: St. Vladimir's Seminary Press), 1987). *The Way of a Pilgrim and The Pilgrim Continues His Way*, Translation by Eleanor French, (Harper Collins Publishers, 1965).

REFLECTION 21

"WALK AS CHILDREN OF LIGHT ..."

If I say, "Surely the darkness shall cover me, and the light around me become night," even the darkness is not dark to you; the night is as bright as the day, for darkness is as light to you.
— Psalm 139:11-12

Read More: 1 Corinthians 15; 2 Corinthians 4:1ff

When I was growing up in Chicago, my Mom and I would wait patiently by our second story apartment window for Dad's car lights to approach. "When will we see the lights?" I asked. Dad was coming home from work. We couldn't wait! When we spotted the car lights ... we would shout, "There's Dad's lights!" In a few seconds we would be re-united as we could hear Dad running up the stairs. Without those car lights we might not have waited and kept watch.

Waiting is the hardest activity for most people in hospitals or doctor's offices. Usually a zillion thoughts are running through their minds. Has that ever happened to you? Will my illness be serious? Is there medication to help ease the pain? Is my doctor competent? Who is walking the dog at home right now? Where did I put my cookbook? I thought my appointment was for 1:30 pm, not 3 pm! I can't stand this waiting ....

If you have ever waited in an emergency room you might have asked yourself: "Why do we have to fill out so many forms? What's all the bother with payment?" Or, "Hey, I'm bleeding over here!" "Forget the forms ... give me some help – now!"

As a child I recall seeing lighthouses on Lake Michigan in Chicago as well as lighthouses on the other great lakes. Not long ago I was traveling in New England. While I was there I fell in love again with the lighthouses.

Along the rocky shore in Portland, Maine stood a strong beacon of hope for those in the waters below. The constant beam of light provided a sense of security. Sometimes ships would end up on the rocks, but most of the time all went smoothly. The lighthouse gave direction and pointed the way to safety. Once in a while one would even hear the fog horns!!

In much the same manner Jesus is our lighthouse. He provides direction and security in our troubled waters. In Jesus, we are safe and secure. When we stand in the light of Jesus, we are exposing ourselves to his love, mercy, and grace. We need not fear the light for in Jesus there is no darkness. As Isaiah says, *"Arise, shine, for your light has come!"* (60:1).

Give me a light, yes, indeed, give me the light of Jesus! Recall the words from the psalmist, "… even the darkness is not dark to you; the night is bright as the day, for darkness is as light with you …" (Psalm 139:12). Go forward into the light of Jesus. He lights our way.

REFLECTION 22

DON'T BLOW YOUR SEWER COVER!

The steadfast love of the Lord never ceases, his mercies never come to an end; they are new every morning; great is your faithfulness.

– Lamentations 3:22-23

Hermosa Beach, California is certainly proud to have a resident named John Hales. Not only is he a gentleman, he is also a scholar, as well as a Hermosa Beach historian. John continues to live in the community which he has called home for more than fifty years. During World War II, John spent three very hot summers in Oklahoma. Ask him what it was like before air conditioning! Do you remember something called "humidity?"

John's extensive career is in advertising, graphic arts, engineering, and dabbling in photography. In 1964 John designed the Hermosa Beach Seal (mosaic in 1965) which currently hangs in the Lobby of the Hermosa Beach City Hall off Pier Avenue. John shared with me the story of the pebbles that surround the design. Those pebbles, John said, are from the many walks he and his late wife, Lorraine, would make along the coast in northern California. John has many fond memories and enjoys telling the story about the pebbles. There is even a barracuda's jawbone among all the pebbles.

The four logos on the Seal are of a cattle brand made by a blacksmith on Olvera Street (see *The Rancho San Pedro*, 1961, by Robert Cameron Gillingham, with information from Antonio Ignacio Avila, 1848 [possible connection with the Adobe Avila] the man who held the land grant to Rancho Sausal Redondo, which encompassed the Hermosa Beach of today); waves representing the ocean; sports equipment, featuring a tennis racquet, baseball bat, and soccer ball; and recreation, represented by a little cottage. The beach has its advantages ... and Hermosa Beach is lovelier with its Hales seal.

John Hales was honored by the Hermosa Beach City Council as they designated the first sewer cover to include John's Hermosa Beach 1964 Seal. The first sewer cover with John's seal is at the end of John's street. The plan calls for most of Hermosa Beach to have John's seal of approval on them!

All of the major newspapers honored John with articles and photographs of the sewer cover: "Designer Sewer Lids Make Southland Debut,"by Bob Pool, *Los Angeles Times*, 2005; "Hermosa Beach Has It Covered When It Comes to Stylish Manholes,"by Deepa Bharath, *Daily Breeze*, 2005; and *The Beach Reporter*, Friday, March 31, 2005.

I also learned that John's father, George Hales, helped with the design of the LA City Hall. I noticed that several mayors, including, James Hahn, signed the design book.

A little birdie told me that the Hermosa Beach Historical Society will be naming one of their historical data rooms after John Hales. John's cover has been blown! Thanks John for your many years of service to the Hermosa Beach community. By the way, for many years John ran 5k & 10k races and his numerous trophies and ribbons stand guard over the Hermosa Beach Seal in his home office. Yeah, John!

Reflection 23

Ecumenical Partners

I therefore, the prisoner in the Lord, beg you to lead a life worthy of the calling to which you have been called, with all humility and gentleness, with patience, bearing with one another in love, making every effort to maintain the unity of the Spirit in the bond of peace. There is one body and one Spirit, just as you were called to the one hope of your calling, one Lord, one faith, one baptism, one God and Father of all, who is above all and through all and in all.

– Ephesians 4:1-6

Not long ago I led worship at the Community Congregational United Church of Christ (UCC), Los Alamitos. The ELCA (Evangelical Lutheran Church in America) is an ecumenical partner with the UCC (www.ucc.org). What is striking about the UCC Los Alamitos Church is the large rose window behind the altar. The large beautiful stained glass ecumenical cross is visible from Katella Avenue and anywhere inside the sanctuary. As you might imagine the light comes pouring through the stained glass and the sanctuary is filled with lots of color!

My Interim Ministry Network mentor for six months, the Rev. Gail Benson, interim pastor at the Los Alamitos church, asked me to lead worship and preach while she and her husband, who is also a UCC pastor, were away.

My introduction to the congregation was during the Lenten season when I attended one of the Bible studies on Isaiah 57:14-15 led by Pastor Benson. The African Bible Study was used. It is a method of study that allows individual reflection on Scripture within a group. Someone reads the passage, then each person selects one word or phrase that speaks to that person. Then someone reads the same passage again from another translation, this time you share how this word or phrase has meaning for you; and finally someone reads the passage again from another translation and this time each person shares what God is calling you to do or say. The study ends with prayer.

The UCC has been using *The New Century Hymnal* since 1995. There are liturgies for Word and Sacrament, Service of the Word, Baptism, Confirmation, Affirmation of Baptism, Morning & Evening Prayer. The hymns cover the church year, from Advent to Pentecost.

An unexpected blessing was a conversation I had with one of the choir members, Jerry Thomason. Jerry shared that he and his wife were good friends with an ELCA Lutheran pastor who was a Navy Chaplain. As Jerry shared the information about this person, especially the part about Long Island, New York, it sounded more and more like my seminary roommate. Sure enough, Jerry knows my old roommate, Jim Nickols.

When Jim Nickols was stationed at the Seal Beach Weapons Department back in the 1980's, he married a daughter of the Los Alamitos congregation, Janelle Osbourne. Jim Nickols is now retired Captain James Nickols, United States Navy Chaplain. Janelle is also a retired Navy chaplain. Jim, Janelle and children Jennifer & Joel, are now living in Williamsburg, Virginia. Jim is serving an ELCA parish in Williamsburg and enjoying it!

Worship was good that Sunday morning and we all recognized that we even have a few doubts, just like Thomas, whose story was the text for that Sunday after Easter. We learned that doubts do not stop faith. Once again our ecumenical partnerships underscore the notion that we are one in Christ and we are connected as brothers and sisters in Christ. Thanks be to God and thanks for our ecumenical partnerships.

Reflection 24

Door to Paradise

Just then a lawyer stood up to test Jesus. "Teacher," he said, "what must I do to inherit eternal life?"

He said to him, "What is written in the law? What do you read there?"

– Luke 10:25-37

Megan McKenna says "all stories are true, some even happened …"

Once upon a time a man said that he would set out on a journey to look for Paradise. He was not satisfied where he was in this little small village. So he began his journey to Paradise. He walked the whole day, took his mat and bread. Before going to sleep he pointed his shoes in the direction he would go tomorrow. Sometime during the evening when the man was sleeping a trickster entered and saw his shoes and thought to himself, *"I will change the direction of these shoes . . . "* Actually the trickster not knowing of the man's intentions pointed his shoes in the same direction the man came from. When the man got up, he ate some bread and then put his shoes on. He walked the whole day and as he approached the little village he said to himself, *"There is Paradise! I have found it!"* He began meeting people who recognized him and he thought that Paradise is a very beautiful place. The man was so excited that he had found Paradise that he decided to stay there the rest of his life. And as the story goes, he lives happily ever after in Paradise.

What if the door to Paradise is always wide open and we walk right past it?

This story was shared by Sharon Hoover, July 23, 2005 at a Thomas Merton seminar at the Center for Spiritual Development, Orange, California.

Reflection 25

Blessings

Blessing of the Hands
No Two Hands are Alike

1. Different shapes & sizes; large and small; fingers are skinny others are wide.

2. Some Art examples: Michaelangelo's David ... hands are large, seem out of proportion; Sistine Chapel ceiling painting by Michaelangelo where God and Adam's fingers almost touch.

3. Basketball players ... Sean Rooks, who played with both the Lakers and Clippers ... big hands. Shaquille O'Neal and Michael Jordan. In baseball, if a person has "soft hands" it means they are good infielders, they handle the baseball without errors.

4. Garrison Keillor, Prairie Home Companion Radio Show ... saw him in person ... very large hands.

5. Pop music ... *I Want to Hold Your Hand* by the Beatles

Internet GOOGLE search – discovered that hospices, hospitals, nursing homes, etc have been doing Blessing of the Hands for years.

Chaplain Tony Biles at Northeast Medical Center, North Concord, NC, is shown giving the hand blessing to nurses and doctors. May 10, 2002, *The Salisbury Post*.

Examples of hymns that could be used during these Blessings:

Precious Lord, Take My Hand. Words by George Allen (1812-1877); music is by Tommy Dorsey (1899-1993).
> Precious Lord, take my hand,
> lead me on let me stand.
> I am tired, I am weak, I am worn.
> Through the storm,
> through the night, lead me on to the light,
> take my hand, precious Lord, lead me home.
>
> When my way grows drear,
> precious Lord, linger near.
> When my life is almost gone,

hear my cry, hear my call, hold my hand lest I fall.
Take my hand, precious Lord, lead me home.

Lord, Take My Hand and Lead Me, Words by Julie Katharina von Hausmann (1826-1901); music by Friedrich Silcher (1789-1860)
>Lord, take my hand and lead me upon life's way;
>direct, protect, and feed me from day to day.
>Without your grace and favor, I go astray;
>So take my hand, O Lord (Savior) and lead the way.

Take My Life, That I May Be, Words and music by Frances R. Havergal (1836-1879)
>Take my hands and let them move
>at the impulse of thy love,
>take my feet and let them be
>swift and beautiful for thee.

» Idea of tracing your hand…then write a word or phrase describing what your hand(s) will do today, for example: greet someone, bless someone, cheer someone, thumbs up …
» Join hands together for a blessing.
» May the work of your hands bring healing to all the people you touch
» May the God who formed these hands guide them to bring the healing touch of life and bless these hands to be instruments of healing.
» Blessings and appreciation for the many tasks these hands do.

>*He's Got the Whole World in His Hands*
>He's got the **whole world** in his hands.
>He's got the **whole world** in his hands.
>He's got the **whole world** in his hands.
>He's got the **whole world** in his hands.

(substitute "whole world" with: wind and rain; little bitty babies; brothers and sisters; everybody here)

BLESSING OF THE HOME

Read: Psalm 46, 136, 141

INTRODUCTION

Matthew writes that when the magi saw the shining star stop overhead, they were filled with joy. "On entering the house, they saw the child with Mary his mother" (Matthew 2:10-11). In the home, Christ is met in family and friends, in visitors and strangers. In the home, faith is shared, nurtured, and put into action. In the home, Christ is welcome.

Twelfth Night (January 5) or another day during the season of Epiphany offers an occasion for gathering with friends and family members for a blessing of the home, using the following as a model. Someone may lead the greeting and blessing, while another person my read the Scripture passage. Following an eastern European tradition, a visual blessing may be inscribed with white chalk above the main door; for example, 20 + CMB + 15. The numbers change with each new year. The three letters stand for either the ancient Latin blessing: *Christe mansionem benedica*, which means, "Christ, bless this house," or the legendary names of the magi (Caspar, Melchior, and Balthasar).

GREETING

May peace be to this house and to all who enter here.
By wisdom a house is built and through understanding it is established; through knowledge its rooms are filled with rare and beautiful treasures.

— Proverbs 24:3-4

READING

As we prepare to ask God's blessing on this household, let us listen to the words of Scripture:

In the beginning was the Word, and the Word was with God, and the Word was God. He was in the beginning with God. All things came into being through him, and without him not one thing came into being. What has come into being in him was life, and the life was the light of all people ... The Word became flesh and lived among us, and we have seen his glory, the glory as of a father's only son, full of grace and truth ... From his fullness we have all received, grace upon grace.

— John 1:1-4, 14, 16

INSCRIPTION

This inscription may be made with chalk above the entrance: 20 + C M B + 15. The magi of old, known as C: Caspar, M:

Melchior, and B: Balthasar followed the star of God's son who came to dwell among us. 20: two thousand. 15: and fifteen years ago. +: Christ, bless this house, +: and remain with us throughout the new year.

Prayer of Blessing

O God, you revealed your Son to all people by the shining light of a star. We pray that you bless this home and all who live here with your gracious presence. May your love be our inspiration, your wisdom our guide, your truth our light and your peace our benediction; through Christ our Lord. Amen.

Source: St. John's Lutheran Church, Orange, California. Bulletin, January 4, 2015, p. 10-11.

Reflection 26

A Chaplain's Grief Reflections: Two Years Later

It has been two years since my wife, Nancy, died (January 3, 2012). I have found support and comfort in a local grief group focusing my feelings on losing the love of my life. My future plans include attending another grief group in order to continue to work on my grieving spirit. **My sense is that grief never ends.** It seems like there is always something or someone to remind me of my dear wife Nancy.

Another source of personal support has come from several seminary classmates, also Lutheran pastors, who live in the area. They have prayed with me and listened to my stories. We have spent much time over breakfast and even a few beers, I might add, reflecting on Nancy and the impact she made on my life. I realize that my life goes on with just a few more twists and turns. In one sense, my life without Nancy is a new chapter in my life.

After the grave marker was in place (before Nancy's April 2012 birthday), I noticed in late May that the marker had started shifting and sinking to the right and was filthy. I shared my observations, including photos, with the mortuary. The marker was re-leveled and cleaned. The mortuary said that sometimes the markers sink and need to be re-leveled. They also re-seeded the grass. I might add that the grave looks much better – as good as can be expected for graves!

My spirit has been enriched by a bagpiper who walks over the sacred grounds every Memorial Day weekend and 4th of July, playing *Amazing Grace* and other bagpipe favorites. Nancy heard the same bagpiper many times! When the bagpiper walked over Nancy's grave this past year playing *Amazing Grace*, it was almost too much for me to bear. It is and has been a heart wrenching experience. The grave marker is another reminder of my own future passing. Seeing your name carved into the stone marker is a call into the future that I will not live forever in my body. The only missing piece is my death date.

When my sister and sister-in-law were here in mid-July, at my request, they went through Nancy's clothes and shoes. I remembered Nancy's words to me and also written in a notebook for me to discover. Nancy said, *"I want you to take several boxes of my clothes to a thrift store in Torrance and Anaheim."* She continued, *"who knows when you will see my clothes walking around Torrance or Anaheim … look for me in the clothes I wore!"* I've been looking but no sightings of Nancy's clothes or shoes in Torrance or Anaheim! Most of her clothes were taken to Goodwill in Anaheim, not far from the house. I'll keep looking for Nancy's clothes and shoes in those cities!

I suppose the most difficult part of my grief is coming home to an empty home. The emptiness and the silence are always present. The memories of Nancy's presence are lasting. However, I am discovering how difficult it is to cook for one person, do all the food shopping, all the laundry (do I really dirty that many clothes?), clean the bathrooms, and make sure the house is presentable when guests arrive! By the way, I still cut the grass, weed the flower beds and trim the trees! I still sense Nancy's presence especially when I spray some of her cologne around the house, just to smell her scent!! I have even put on a few pieces of her jewelry, mostly necklaces, to remind me of her beauty.

I discovered that Nancy left several three-ring binders with instructions on how to use the new front loading washing machine. She included diagrams and reminders for me to be sure to drain the front loader after I was done with several loads of laundry! I have found other instructions throughout the house. Nancy lives on in the notes, diagrams, and of course, memories. She would always ask me, *"Did you read the instructions, Charles?" "Yes, Nancy, I've been reading the instructions!"* Thanks for caring for me beyond the grave!

I find that my mind and my dreams take me back to the year 2005 when Nancy had a resection of her colon. (Resource: *On Grief and Grieving* by Elisabeth Kübler-Ross and David Kessler, see the Introduction on "Anticipatory Grief," 1-5). Prior to the resection, she had some bleeding from her colon. A colonoscopy revealed polyps. At the time of the resection I recall the physician saying, *"We got it all ... we're going to beat this."* No chemotherapy was needed at that time. Nancy was "good to go!" 40-50 lymph nodes were removed and Nancy had an annual colonoscopies to check for cancer growth.

In the middle of 2009 it was discovered that the cancer had spread to her liver, covering about 40% of her liver, as well as small signs of metastases to her lungs. She began her journey with chemotherapy in the Fall of 2009. She continued to receive chemotherapy for two years. She also continued working full time. The liver tumor did shrink, however the cancer in her lungs continued to grow.

In June of 2011, Nancy decided to go on medical leave/disability from her job at Sakura Finetek, Inc. It was always her intention and goal to return to the job she loved when she was stronger. In July she started some radiation treatments along with on-going chemotherapy. Needless to say the treatments were not working. Nancy continued losing weight and was fatigued. The cancer continued to grow. After receiving the recommendation from her oncologist that hospice would be appropriate, she decided in late November to explore hospice care. In early December several hospice agencies were interviewed and a choice was made. Nancy was now on hospice in late December 2011.

Christmas was approaching and Nancy's family (sister and mother from Phoenix) planned to visit. The four of us had a good Christmas and New Year. It would be the last one for the four of us. All during this time Nancy continued to pay bills and write checks. She even managed to have Christmas presents for each of us. She was surprised when a new Green Bay Packer shirt was among her gifts.

It was obvious that Nancy was getting weaker. She was sleeping more and eating less. She seemed less interested in keeping up with the news. It seemed like she was withdrawing from her family ... she was getting ready to make the transition. She received continuous care the last three days of her life. She was on oxygen and the caregiver from hospice turned her every two hours. She was comfortable and not in pain. The one request from Nancy was to see all the angels (figurines) we had in the house. I brought them to the bedroom and put them on the bookcases overlooking her bed. The angels were present; they were watching. Her room was a holy space. The angels were nearby; they surrounded her bed.

In July when Nancy started her disability leave, she reminded me that she thought she would not be around for her birthday in

April 2012. Nancy died peacefully on January 3, surrounded by her husband, sister, and mother. She slipped away peacefully, with the angels she wanted in her room.

Shortly after she died I happened to look out the bedroom window and observed what seemed to be a beautiful Monarch butterfly fluttering near the window. The butterfly seemed to stay there forever. For Christians, the butterfly is a symbol of the resurrection, the transformation from this life to the next. The transformation is going from what we know to what we do not know. We are changed into our new life forms. Nancy is in God's hands, always was and always will be, now and forever.

Funny thing about those butterflies, I see them all the time around the house, and not just in the back yard near the window. Now they seem to be by the front door entrance and even trying to enter the side garage door. I sense God is telling me something. Hold on to the memories of your loved ones and give thanks to God for life! We will all be transformed in the twinkling of an eye into God's great plan. Rejoice and give thanks to God!!

Finally, here are some resources I have found helpful these past two years: *The Essential Guide to Grief and Grieving* by Debra Holland; Kenneth Haugk's *Journeying Through Grief*, a series of four booklets; *How To Go On Living When Someone You Love Dies* by Therese Rando; and a classic text, *Good Grief* by Granger Westberg. Happy reading and God bless your time of grief.

Reflection 27

The Puddle Fish

A story as heard by the Rev. Charles J Lopez, Jr

　　Once upon a time in a place far away there lived lots of fish in a little puddle. The puddle fish knew their way around the puddle and every day they would wait for the waterbugs to show up on the surface of the water.

　　When the waterbugs arrived the puddle fish would announce, "It's time to eat!"

　　They were content with their little puddle surroundings and knew all the other fish in the puddle. They swam in circles day after day.

　　One day this beautiful rainbow fish appeared.

　　The puddle fish wanted to know where and how the rainbow fish managed to find their little puddle.

"I came from the sea, far from this puddle," the rainbow fish said. "I swam from the sea to the river and then to this puddle."

The puddle fish all looked the same and so this rainbow fish was fascinating to the puddle fish. The puddle fish liked their puddle and did not want to leave.

"In the sea there are many places to swim and explore. You don't need to swim around in circles like you do in this puddle," the rainbow fish declared.

The rainbow fish asked if any of the puddle fish would like to hear about the sea.

Most of the puddle fish said, "No."

However, one puddle fish that stuttered swam up to the rainbow fish and asked, "Where ... Where did you say you came from?"

The rainbow fish said, "From the sea."

The stuttering fish said, "Why, that's that's too too far for me. Besides, we pudd-le pudd-le fish know our surroundings and the big sea would be too big for us pudd-le fish. How do you get to the sea from this puddle?"

"Oh, that's easy! You just jump from this puddle to the river and the river carries you out to the sea."

"I don't know if I want to go to the sea," said the stuttering puddle fish, "I like my puddle just fine."

Then the rainbow fish said something that made the puddle fish get very scared. "It's summer now, and the puddle you're swimming in won't last forever. In fact, it *will* dry up soon."

The puddle fish wondered about their surroundings. Would they need to jump from the puddle to the river and finally end up in the big sea?

"I'm going back to the sea. Anyone want to go with me?" said the rainbow fish.

"I'll try!" the puddle fish who stuttered said. And off they went! Jumping from the puddle to the river, and eventually ending up at the sea.

Reflection 28

Madonna With Child

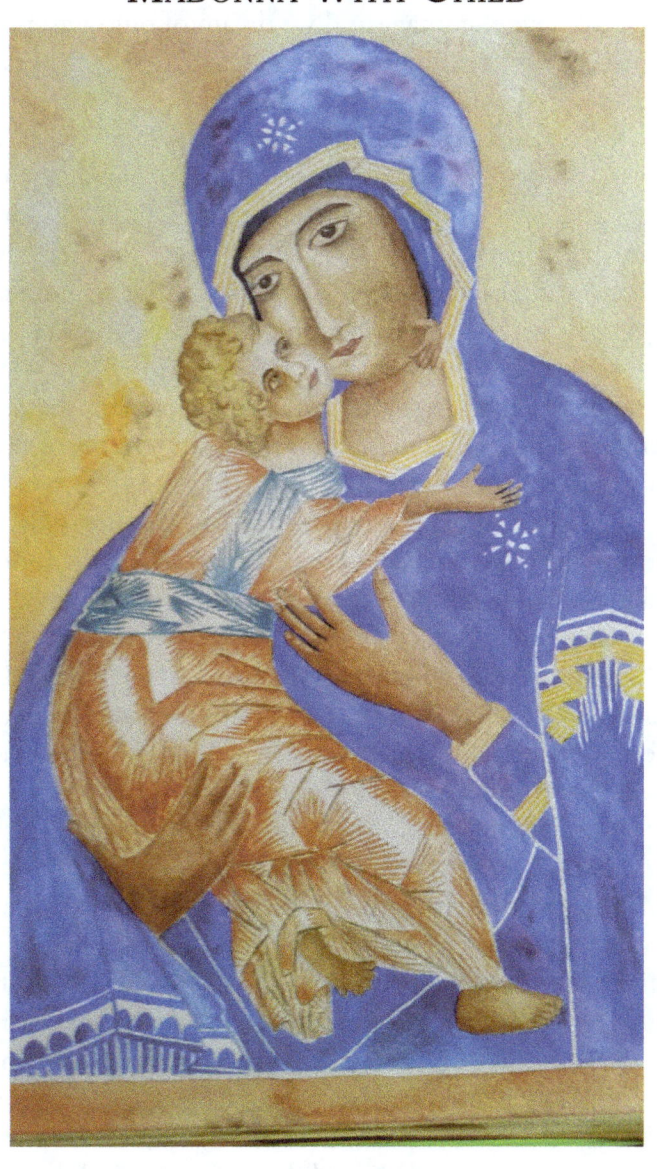

All the great art masters seem to have produced their version of the Madonna with child. Do you have a favorite? I always enjoyed Raphael's *Madonna of the Chair*. Mary holding the baby Jesus is precious. We love the image and we dream of our own mothers. I am writing this reflection on Mother's Day. There is a special bond between mothers' and their children.

My mother, Wilma Pauline Lopez (née Steinhauer), died in 2009. On this day of celebration for mothers, I am aware that my thoughts and dreams have been centered on Mom. What makes it worse, or perhaps better, is my ministry as a hospice chaplain. I am discovering the emotional strain when my assignment is to visit a person who is about the same age as my mother and that person is dying.

I recall being with my mom before she died. She squeezed my hand even though she could no longer talk to me or my sister. She died peacefully the next morning. I have confessed to hospice family members that my mother died recently. In the midst of their anticipatory grief, some have provided a human caring for me. It is marvelous to know that we have feelings and that the love for our mothers is apparent.

I am reminded of Michelangelo's *Pieta*, where the dead Jesus is in Mary's lap (John 19:25-42). It is a serene and gracious sculpture. As one author has said, "perhaps she is praying rather than looking at the body of her dear son." Whatever the image is for you, it definitely leaves a lasting impression. Mothers and their children are connected.

Mary loved her son, Jesus. Jesus loved his mother, Mary. The two are connected in the story. We only have one biological mother and father. When they die, we have a sense of being an orphan (cf. John 14:18). Someone once wrote that when both parents are dead, the child is free. We are at one and the same time orphaned and free. John's Gospel (John 15) reminds us that *"Jesus is the vine, we are the branches"* (John 15:5). We are connected with Jesus and never alone. As Jesus promised, the Holy Spirit is here. (John 14:26ff).

When a child is separated from their mother or father, it seems that the child will search for their parent until they find a path that connects them. On this day, let us rejoice with all the mothers of the world. Let us give thanks to God for their love and kindness. May the lessons we learned from our mothers be a reflection of how we show love and kindness to our own children and to children of the world.

Finally, there is this story:

A little girl came home from a neighbor's house where her little friend had died. Her father asked her gently why she had gone. The child replied that she went to make her friend's mother feel better.

"And what could you do to make her feel better?" asked her father.

"I climbed into her lap and cried with her."

(*Preaching on Death: An Ecumenical Resource,* (The Liturgical Conference, Silver Spring, MD, 1997), p. 95)

Appendix A

Decisions at the End of Life, Part 1

> *No, in all these things we are more than conquerors through him who loved us. For I am convinced that neither death, nor life, nor angels, nor rulers, nor things present, nor things to come, nor powers, nor height, nor depth, nor anything else in all creation, will be able to separate us from the love of God in Christ Jesus our Lord.*
>
> *— Romans 8:37-39*

The other day, I read an interesting reflection by Chaplain Peter Mallin, Spiritual Care Department at Little Company of Mary Hospice, Torrance, California. Someone asked him how they can begin talking with their loved one about end of life decisions. Chaplain Mallin said, "These can be really difficult discussions, but talking about these things is one of the most life giving things you can do." He then shared **five guidelines** for talking about end of life decisions.

» **Think about the goal.** What are you trying to accomplish by your medical decisions – longer life, a return home, pain-free death? What decisions need to be made to reach that goal? Do you have an Advanced Directive? Are there things that your relative(s) need to "get done" before you die?

» **Speak from your gut.** These discussions can produce lots of emotions. Be honest about how you really feel. "I think she is dying." "I'm scared." "I love you." "We need some help making these decisions." Be sensitive to your loved ones, but be honest with yourself and others.

» **Take time to go back.** Spend some time doing a **"life review."** A person who is dying may want to think about their past – their successes and failures, hopes and dreams. Sit and listen to

stories and memories. Allow a person's past to give you a picture of what's valuable to them for the future.
» **Draw close to God.** We are spiritual people. We may have spiritual, through may be not religious, thoughts as we approach death. Some may want clergy or specific religious rituals, others may see family or nature as spiritually supportive. Find out what would help them to **"get centered."**
» **Remember to be gracious.** Emotions will be strong during this time. There will be stress, frustrations, fears, and sadness. **Be gentle** with yourself and others, especially as family and friends comes together. This is a special time, but difficult time. Remember to take care of yourself in all of this.

DECISIONS AT THE END OF LIFE, PART 2

"I am the Alpha and the Omega, the first and the last, the beginning and the end."

— Revelation 22:13

The names of Karen Ann Quinlan, Nancy Cruzan and Terri Schiavo come to mind when end of life issues are raised. Nation and local debates have been sparked, the U.S. Government has played a role, and the media has documented the unfolding of these difficult and painful issues. What about Living Wills and Power of Attorney? Will you ever need them?

Here are a few suggestions regarding a Living Will and a Durable Power of Attorney (DPOA). Each person, in consultation with their family, needs to specify whether you wish to be resuscitated or not. Make it absolutely clear whether you wish to be kept alive with a feeding tube.

Discuss these issues with whichever doctor is closest to you (or most likely to be there when you are desperately ill), how much "heroic" or unusual treatment you want and for how long it should be continued. Indicate, in no uncertain terms, if and when you wish to be resuscitated.

Responsive Reading:

People: We receive the strength offered by our Creator.

Leader: Let us receive the vision to see with the eyes of our hearts.

People: And the courage to persevere in difficult times.

Leader: May all whose lives we touch come to know God's love.

People: May that same love be a consolation to us.

Leader: Let us return to our duties with blessed hands that are attentive, healing, meticulous, reliable, and hard-working.

People: We go, renewed and refreshed, ready to imagine peace in new ways.

Appendix B

Directives for End of Life

FULL NAME:

DATE & PLACE OF BIRTH:

DATE OF BAPTISM:

DATE OF CONFIRMATION:

DATE OF MARRIAGE:

CHILDREN:

STREET ADDRESS:

CITY/STATE: ZIP:

TELEPHONE(S):

EMAIL:

RESPONSIBLE PARTY #1:

RESPONSIBLE PARTY #2:

I. ADVANCED DIRECTIVES

I have given "Durable Power of Attorney for Healthcare."

NAME & PHONE NUMBER OF AGENT:

    I have completed a Living Will.

    I have completed a "Contribution of Anatomical Gift" form.

Give copies of the above forms to Responsible Party.

    I have included family/friends in my Will/Estate.

II. GUIDE TO FUNERAL PLANNING

I direct that, at my death, the following is to occur, if it all possible.

Mortuary Name, Address & Telephone:

Cemetery (Earth Burial):

Above ground Burial(Mausoleum):

Graveside only:

Cremation (Name, Address, Telephone of Crematorium):

Ashes to be Scattered?   Where:

Ashes to be buried in above noted Cemetery?

    I am interested in being interred in a columbarium, which is a wall located in a Memorial Garden containing niches for the interment of ashes (cremains).

Special Instructions for Worship/Liturgy

Memorial Service (casket not present)

Funeral Service (casket present)   Open casket   Closed casket

Location

Reception Location

2 of my favorite hymns

2 of my favorite Scriptures/Bible stories/Bible characters

Other instructions: Organist/Soloist

Suggestions for Memorial Gifts

Brief biographical notes for Obituary/Sermon notes

Today's Date: **Signature:**

Appendix C

The Affordable Care Act

Confusion, exchanges, marketplace, affordable care, transparency, fee for service, Cadillac plan, public plan, rationed care ... these are terms we will come to live with now and in the future. Steven Brill in a Special Report in *Time*, "Bitter Pill: How outrageous pricing and egregious profits are destroying our health care," (p. 16-55 in *Time* magazine, March 4, 2013), says that "the U.S. is likely to spend $2.8 trillion this year on health care" (p. 20, www.time.com).

Kate Pickert writes in a *Time* magazine article, "What Health-Care Reform Really Means" (August 10, 2013, p.32-33) that "the U.S. spends more on health care than any other country and yet ranks behind 18 other industrialized nations in medically preventable deaths." Furthermore, Pickert says that "53% are insured through an employer; 5% are insured independently; 26% are insured through a public program; 62% are the owner of a small business; and 15% are uninsured ..." (p.32-33)

In a recent *Parade* health care update (www.parade.com, Sunday, October 27, 2013, p. 21), Frank Lalli, indicates that individuals have until March 31, 2014, to sign up for insurance under the **Affordable Care Act**, but for coverage starting January 1, enroll by mid-December. Regardless of when you sign up, benefits run through the end of 2014. Go to www.healthcare.gov or call 800-318-2596 (Health Insurance Marketplace) to connect with your state's public exchange, where you can shop for insurance and find out whether you qualify for subsidies or even Medicaid. Remember, says Frank Lalli, nearly everyone must get health insurance next year or face a fine of $95 or 1 percent of their income – whichever is greater. But if you already have a decent plan, say, through work, you don't need to buy more insurance.

It all sounds so good. Unfortunately we all know that the government was shut down for the first sixteen days in October 2013. In addition, www.healthcare.gov crashed on October 1st with too many users trying to access the site and find out about the **Affordable Care Act** exchanges, marketplace, etc. The phrase that flashes across the screen is: "The system is down at the moment." Kathleen Sebelius, Secretary for Health & Human Services, says she is to blame for the debacle with the website. Now the promise is that the website will be fixed by November 30th (*Orange County Register*, Saturday, October 26, 2013, p.3). Perhaps you are asking: Who do you believe and what will happen next? *The Los Angeles Times*, Sunday, November 3, 2013, p. A34 points out that "… the one thing Americans agree on: they want a government that solves problems, not creates them."

Author Kate Pickert in *Time* magazine (November 11, 2013, p.12) has assembled some talking points from speeches by President Barack Obama: On October 7, 2008 …'let me just repeat, if you've got a health care plan that you like, you can keep it.' On June 15, 2009 … 'that means that no matter how we reform health care, we will keep this promise to the American people: If you like your doctor, you will be able to keep your doctor, period. If you like your health care plan, you'll be able to keep your health care plan, period. No one will take it away, no matter what.' On March 3, 2010 … 'if you like your plan, you can keep your plan.' On September 29, 2010… 'there's nothing in the bill that says you have to change the health insurance that you've got right now.' On June 28, 2012 … 'if you're one of the more than 250 million Americans who already have health insurance, you will keep your health insurance.'

The problem, of course, is that insurance companies change their policies all the time. Millions were kicked off their plans every year even before the **Affordable Care Act**. There will be changes now because some existing policies do not meet the **Affordable Care Act** minimums. Perhaps the President spoke too soon and should have known better and kept silent. Perhaps there is no quick fix.

On January 1, 2014, President Barack Obama's **Affordable Care Act** (ACA) will greatly expand the health care benefits being offered to the 55 million Americans with no health coverage, says Frank Lalli, in "The Affordable Care Act & You" (*AARP The Magazine*, August/September 2013, p. 26 ff, www.aarp.org/magazine. There are ten essential health benefits: ambulatory patient services, prescription drugs, emergency care, mental health services, hospitalization, rehabilitative services, preventive and wellness services, laboratory services, pediatric care, and maternity and newborn care. Lalli says that "the law states that it eliminates lifetime limits on essential medical expenses; it prohibits insurers from dropping your coverage or raising your premiums if you get sick – or from denying coverage if you have a preexisting condition; it ensures that your child can stay on your health plan until age 26; and it caps annual out-of-pocket medical and drug expenses up to an estimated $6,400 for individuals and $12,800 for families." Another resource to learn more about the ACA is www.healthlawanswers.org, also try www.webMD.com.

Where this will end or what it will look like is hard to say. For pastors, rabbis, imams in churches, synagogues or mosques or chaplains in hospitals/hospices, military or in specialized ministries, the idea is certainly to go slow. Be aware of the needs of those around your place of employment.

Certainly the words from the Prophets of the Hebrew Scriptures will awaken all to the need to be aware of the poor and vulnerable around us. Matthew's Gospel also applies, that is, serving the "least of these" is most appropriate (Matthew 25). Those in religious life come in all shapes and sizes, and opinions will vary from church to church, synagogue to synagogue, mosque to mosque. One size does not fit all in this case.

What is apparent is that those who have no healthcare coverage may now have that opportunity to be covered. I saw several quotes the other day from Walter W. Borginis III in a magazine titled *Caring*, June 2013, pp. 44-45, "Congress can't cut our caring attitude or our spirit" and "Americans are capable of doing great things, and the truest measure of our success is how we take care of our most vulnerable members." (www.nahc.org. *Caring* is a publication of the National Association for Home Care & Hospice).

Caring for the poor and most vulnerable is what we all need to consider as we move forward with the **Affordable Care Act**. One never knows when we, too, might be faced with being one of the most vulnerable.

APPENDIX D

ELDER ABUSE

As a hospice chaplain and parish pastor I have witnessed abuse. Child and Elder abuse seem to be on the rise these days. Clergy are always looking for information. Who do you call when you experience elder or child abuse? Here is some information for both Los Angeles and Orange counties. Look for similar agencies in your state and county.

Clergy have been mandated reporters for child abuse since January 1996. (See paragraphs 11165ff. See West's Annotated California Codes. Penal Code, Sections 4400-11999.) The Official California Penal Code Classification is published by the West Group, 2000. (editor@westgroup.com and home page: www.westgroup.com). Child Protective Services (CPS) in Orange County 714-940-1000; in Los Angeles County 800-540-4000.

As of January 2003 clergy are now mandatory reporters for Elder Abuse. Please consult, West's Annotated California Codes. Welfare & Institutions Code, Sections 15300-17699. See paragraphs 15600ff, especially 15630. Official California Welfare & Institutions Code Classification, published by the West Group, 2001 (editor@westgroup.com and home page: www.westgroup.com). One does not need proof of abuse, only suspecting abuse would prompt one to report. Adult Protective Services (APS) toll-free numbers: Los Angeles County 1-877-477-3646; Orange County 1-800-451-5155.

Some helpful information for Elder Abuse Clergy Mandatory reporting:
» Eldercare, see.www.aoa.gov. which is the Administration on Aging.

- » Elder locator, 1-800-677-1166. Services for county/city. Operated 24 hours a day/7 days a week. Alzheimer's hotline, 1-800-621-0379.
- » Sometimes people ask: How do I find a Nursing Home? The information is in Spanish, Chinese, and English. Go to www.medicare.gov. Look up Nursing Home and click on inspection results. Every nursing home is required by law to submit to an annual inspection report. The results are public knowledge.
- » Ombudsman – always serves as an advocate for the patient, 1-800-334-9473
- » All *un*licensed facility complaints go to APS = Adult Protective Services, Los Angeles County 1-877-477-3646. All *licensed* facilities complaints go to the local Ombudsman.
- » Voluntary Reporters – can be anonymous. Mandated Reporters – must identify themselves when reporting.
- » LA for Seniors, Elders 65+ go to: www.LA4seniors.com. Information is available in Armenian, Chinese, Japanese, Korean, Filipino, Russian, Spanish, Yiddish, and English.
- » Another helpful website is: www.wiseseniorservices.org
- » Orange County Information Line: 888-600-4357 (8:30 am -4:40 pm) or www.infolinkoc.org.
- » Providence TrinityCare Hospice Referral 1-800-535-8446 (M-F 9:00 am – 5:00 pm). www.trinitycarehospice.org

More Resources

Adams, M.D., Patch with Mylander, Maureen. *Gesundheit. Bringing Good Health to You, the Medical System, and Society through Physician Service, Complementary Therapies, Humor, and Joy.* (Rochester, Vermont: Healing Arts Press, 1993, 1998). In addition in DVD, Robin Williams, *Patch Adams*. Universal City, CA: Universal Studios, 1999.

Aesop's Fables. Introduction and Notes by D.L. Ashliman. NY: Barnes & Noble Classics, 2003.

Ahronheim, Judith and Weber, Doron. *Final Passages: Positive Choices for the Dying and their Loved Ones*. New York: Simon & Schuster, 1992.

Albom, Mitch. *Tuesdays with Morrie*. NY: Doubleday, 1997.

_____. *The Five People You Meet in Heaven*. NY: Hyperion, 2003.

Allsopp, Michael E., ed. *Models of Christian Ethics*. Scranton: The University of Scranton Press, 2003.

Anderson, Megory. *Sacred Dying: Creating Rituals for Embracing the End of Life*. Revised and Expanded edition. NY: Marlowe & Company, 2001, 2003.

Appleton, George, ed. *The Oxford Book of Prayers*. Oxford: Oxford University Press, 1985.

Aristotle. *Nicomachean Ethics*. Translated with introduction, notes, and glossary, by Terence Irwin. Indianapolis, Indiana: Hackett Publishing Company, 1985.

American Pain Society Home Page: http://www.ampainsoc.org. "Total Pain: The Work of Cicely Saunders and the Hospice Movement." Accessed November 15, 2012.

Armstrong, Karen. *Islam: A Short History*. Revised and Updated. NY: Modern Library, 2000, 2002.

_____. *The Battle for God*. NY: Ballantine Books, 2000)

_____. *Jerusalem: One City, Three Faiths.* NY: Alfred A. Knopf, 1996.

_____. *The Bible: A Biography.* NY: Grove Press, 2007.

Ashenburg, Katherine. *The Mourner's Dance: What We Do When People Die.* New York: North Point Press. A Division of Farrar, Straus and Giroux, 2002.

Association for Death Education and Counseling. "Elisabeth Kübler-Ross Dies," The Forum, October/November/December 2004, 2005.

Bane, J. Donald, Kutscher, Austin H., Neale, Robert E., and Reeves, Robert B. Jr., eds. *Death and Ministry: Pastoral Care of the Dying and the Bereaved.* NY: The Seabury Press, 1975.

Barks, Coleman, with A.J. Arberry and Nevit Ergin, trans. *Rumi: Bridge to the Soul: Journeys Into the Music and Silence of the Heart.* Harper Collins, 2007.

Barry, William A. *God & You. Prayer as a Personal Relationship.* NY: Paulist Press, 1987.

_____. *Paying Attention to God.* Notre Dame, Indiana: Ave Maria Press, 1990.

_____. *Letting God Come Close: An Approach to the Ignatian Spiritual Exercises.* Chicago: Loyola Press, 2001.

Barry, William A. and Connolly, William J. *The Practice of Spiritual Direction*, Second Edition, Revised. New York: Harper Collins Publishers, 1982.

Becker, Ernest. *The Denial of Death.* NY: The Free Press, 1973.

Bennett, Amanda and Foley, Terence B. *In Memoriam: A Practical Guide to Planning A Memorial Service.* NY: A Fireside Book. Published by Simon & Schuster, 1997.

Beresford, Larry. *The Hospice Handbook: A Complete Guide.* Boston: Little, Brown and Company, 1993.

Bernanos, Georges. *The Diary Of A Country Priest.* NY: Image Books, 1954.

Berra, Yogi with Kaplan, Dave. *When You Come To A Fork in the Road, Take It!* NY: Hyperion, 2001.

Biddle, Perry H. Jr. *A Hospital Visitation Manual.* Grand Rapids, MI: William E. Eerdmans Publishing Company, Revised & Updated, 1994.

Binkewicz, Matthew P. *Peaceful Journey: A Hospice Chaplain's Guide to End of Life.* Ithaca, NY: Paramount Market Publishing, Inc. 2005.

Blair, Robert. *The Funeral and Wedding Handbook.* Second Edition. Lima, Ohio: CSS Publishing Company, Inc., 2001.

Blake, Donald S. *Mary Aikenhead: Servant of the Poor, Founder of the Religious Sisters of Charity.* Dublin: Caritas, 2001.

Borg, Marcus J. *Jesus: Uncovering The Life, Teachings, and Relevance of A Religious Revolutionary.* Harper One, 2006.

_____. *Jesus A New Vision: Spirit, Culture, and the Life of Discipleship.* Harper San Francisco, 1987.

_____. *Reading the Bible Again for the First Time: Taking the Bible Seriously but Not Literally.* Harper San Francisco, 2001.

_____. *Meeting Jesus Again for the First Time: The Historical Jesus & the Heart of Contemporary Faith.* Harper San Francisco, 1994),

_____. *The God We Never Knew: Beyond Dogmatic Religion To a More Authentic Contemporary Faith.* Harper San Francisco, 1997.

_____, ed. *Jesus at 2000.* WestviewPress, 1997.

_____. *The Heart of Christianity: Rediscovering A Life of Faith.* Harper San Francisco, 2003.

Borg, Marcus and John Dominic Crossan. *The First Christmas: What the Gospels Really Teach About Jesus's Birth.* Harper One, 2007.

Boyd, Gregory A. *Is God to Blame?: Beyond Pat Answers to the Problem of Suffering.* Downers Grove, IL: InterVarsity Press, 2003.

Brener, Anne. *Mourning & Mitzvah: A Guided Journal for Walking the Mourner's Path Through Grief to Healing*. Woodstock, VT: Jewish Lights Publishing, 1993.

Brenner, Paul R. "Spirituality in Hospice. The Challenge of Success." Bulletin. Chicago: The Park Ridge Center for the Study of Health, Faith, and Ethics. May/June 2001.

Brother Roger of Taize. *God is Love Alone*. Chicago: GIA Publications, Inc. 2001, 2003.

Brody, Jane. *Jane Brody's Guide to the Great Beyond. A Practical Primer to Help You and Your Loved Ones Prepare Medically, Legally, and Emotionally for the End of Life*. New York: Random House, 2009.

Brokering, Herbert. *I'm Thinking of You: Spiritual Letters of Hope and Healing*. Minneapolis: Augsburg, 1996.

Brother Lawrence. *The Practice of the Presence of God*. Springdale, Pennsylvania: Whitaker House, 1982.

Brown, Raymond E. *The Death of the Messiah*. 2 volumes. NY: Doubleday, 1994.

Buchwald, Art. *Too Soon To Say Goodbye*. New York: Random House, 2006.

Buckingham, Robert W. *The Complete Hospice Guide*. NY: Harper & Row, Publishers, 1983.

Burns, George. *100 Years 100 Stories*. NY: G.P. Putnam's Sons, 1996.

Bush, George W. *41: A Portrait of my Father*. NY: Crown Publishers, 2014.

Byock, Ira. *Dying Well: Peace and Possibilities at the End of Life*. New York: Riverhead Books, 1997.

_____. *The Four Things That Matter Most: A Book About Living*. New York: Free Press, 2004.

_____. *The Best Care Possible*. New York: Avery, a member of Penguin Group, 2013. Also see, www.dyingwell.org.

Callanan, Maggie and Kelley, Patricia. *Final Gifts: Understanding the Special Awareness, Needs, and Communications of the Dying.* NY: Bantam Books, 1997.

Callanan, Maggie. *Final Journeys: A Practical Guide for Bringing Care and Comfort at the End of Life.* NY: Bantam Books, 2008.

Carter, Jimmy. *Our Endangered Values: America's Moral Crisis.* NY: Simon & Schuster, 2005.

Clinebell, Howard, *Basic Types of Pastoral Care and Counseling.* New Haven: Yale University, 1983.

Cohen, Kenneth P. *Hospice Prescription for Terminal Care.* Germantown, MD: Aspen Systems Corporation, 1979.

Collett, Merrill. *At Home with Dying: A Zen Hospice Approach.* Boston: Shambhala, 1999.

Collins, Michael. *Francis: Bishop of Rome: A Short Biography.* Collegeville, MN: The Liturgical Press, 2013.

Confessions. Saint Augustine. Translated by Maria Boulding, O.S.B. NY: Vintage Books, 1997.

Cousins, Norman. *Anatomy of an Illness as Perceived by the Patient: Reflections on Healing and Regeneration.* NY: Bantam Books, 1979. First Norton paperback, 2005. Anniversary edition.

Craig, William Lane and Walter Sinott-Armstrong. *God?: A Debate Between a Christian and an Atheist.* Point/Counterpoint Series, James P. Sterba, series ed. Oxford University Press, 2004.

Crossan, John Dominic. *Jesus: A Revolutionary Biography.* Harper San Francisco, 1994)

_____. *The Historical Jesus: The Life of a Mediterranean Jewish Peasant.* Harper San Francisco, 1991.

_____. *The Essential Jesus: What Jesus Really Taught.* Harper San Francisco, 1994, 1995.

Cunningham, Lawrence S., ed. *Thomas Merton, Spiritual Master: The Essential Writings.* New York: Paulist Press, 1992.

Darling, Frank C. *Biblical Healing: Hebrew and Christian Roots.* Boulder, CO: Vista Publications, 1989.

Didion, Joan. *The Year of Magical Thinking.* New York: Alfred A. Knopf, 2005.

Doka, Kenneth J, with Morgan, John D, ed. *Death and Spirituality.* Amityville, NY: Baywood Publishing Company, Inc, 1993.

Dossey, Larry. *Healing Words: The Power of Prayer and the Practice of Medicine.* Harper San Francisco, 1993.

DuBose, Edwin R. "A Special Report: Spiritual Care at the End of Life: Challenges for Hospital, Hospice, and Congregational Clergy." *Second Opinion.* Number 10, April 2002.

DuBose, Edwin R. "Preparing for Death: Linking Medicine, Spirituality, and End-of-Life Care." *Bulletin.* Chicago: The Park Ridge Center for the Study of Health, Faith, and Ethics, May/June, 2001.

Duclow, Donald F. "Dying Well from the Fifteenth Century to Hospice." *Lutheran Quarterly.* Volume 28, Number 2, Summer 2014, 125-148.

Dunn, Hank. *Hard Choices For Loving People: CPR, Artificial Feeding, Comfort Care, and the Patient with a Life-Threatening Illness,* Fourth Edition. Lansdowne, VA: A&A Publishers, Inc., 2007.

Dunn, Bill and Leonard, Kathy. *Through A Season of Grief: Devotions for Your Journey From Mourning to Joy.* Nelson Books, 2004.

Egeberg, Gary. *The Pocket Guide to Prayer.* Minneapolis: Augsburg, 1999.

Edwards, Tilden. *Spiritual Friend: Reclaiming the Gift of Spiritual Direction.* Mahwah, NJ: Paulist Press, 1980.

Engle, Paul E., ed. *Baker's Funeral Handbook: Resources for Pastors.* Grand Rapids, MI: Baker Books, 1996.

Family Handbook of Hospice Care, The. Minneapolis: Fairview Press, 1999.

Farley, Margaret A. *A Framework for Christian Sexual Ethics*. NY: Continuum International Publishing Group, 2006. Reprinted 2011, 2012.

Fitchett, George. *Assessing Spiritual Needs*. Minneapolis: Augsburg Fortress, 1993.

Fitzgerald, Helen. *The Mourning Handbook: The Most Comprehensive Resource Offering Practical and Compassionate Advice on Coping with All Aspects of Death and Dying*. NY: A Fireside Book. Published by Simon & Schuster 1994.

Forell, George Wolfgang. *The Protestant Faith*. Philadelphia: Fortress Press, 1960,1975.

Fowler, James W. *Becoming Adult, Becoming Christian: Adult Development and Christian Faith*. San Francisco: Harper & Row, Publishers, 1984.

_____. *Stages of Faith. The Psychology of Human Development and the Quest for Meaning*. NY: Harper Collins Publishers, 1995.

Friedrich, M.J. "Hospice Care in the United States: A Conversation with Florence S. Wald." *Journal of the American Medical Association*, May 12, 1999, Volume 281, No. 18.

Friedman, Edwin H. *Generation to Generation: Family Process in Church and Synagogue*. NY: The Guilford Press, 1985.

Gaiser, Frederick J. *Healing in the Bible: Theological Insights for Christian Ministry*. Grand Rapids, MI: Baker Academic, 2010.

Girzone, Joseph F. *A Portrait of Jesus*. NY: Doubleday, 1998.

Goleman, Daniel. *Emotional Intelligence*. NY: Bantam Books, 1995, 1997.

Gomez, Jose H. *A Will to Live: Clear Answers on End of Life Issues*. Dallas, TX: Basilica Press, 2006, reprinted 2012.

Gomez, Jose H. *Immigration and the Next America: Renewing the Soul of Our Nation*. Huntington, IN: Our Sunday Visitor Publishing Division, 2013.

Gomez, Medardo Ernesto. *Fire Against Fire*. Minneapolis: Augsburg, 1989. Original publication in Spanish, *Fuego contra Fuego*.

Graham, Billy. *The Heaven Answer Book*. Nashville: Thomas Nelson, 2012.

Graham, Billy. *Nearing Home: Life, Faith, and Finishing Well*. Nashville: Thomas Nelson, 2011.

Grollman, Earl A, ed. *Concerning Death: A Practical Guide for the Living*. Boston: Beacon Press, 1974.

Grudem, Wayne A. Elliot Grudem, editor. *Christian Beliefs: Twenty Basics Every Christian Should Know*. Grand Rapids, MI: Zondervan, 2005.

Guenther, Margaret. "Companions At The Threshold: Spiritual Direction with the Dying." Chapter 8, pp.105-118. Norvene Vest, ed, *Still Listening: New Horizons in Spiritual Direction*. Harrisburg, PA: Morehouse Publishing, 2000.

Guenther, Margaret. *Holy Listening: The Art of Spiritual Direction*. Cambridge, MA: Cowley Publications, 1992.

_____. *Toward Holy Ground: Spiritual Directions for the Second Half of Life*. Cambridge, MA: Cowley Publications, 1995.

Hanh, Thich Nhat. *No Death, No Fear: Comforting Wisdom for Life*. NY: Riverhead Books, 2002.

Hart, Thomas N. *The Art of Christian Listening*. New York: Paulist Press, 1980.

Harter, Michael, ed. *Hearts on Fire: Praying with Jesuits*. Chicago: Loyola Press, 1993, 2004.

Hauerwas, Stanley. *God, Medicine, and Suffering*. Grand Rapids, MI: William B. Eerdmans Publishing Company, 1990.

Haugk, Kenneth C. *Don't Sing Songs To a Heavy Heart: How to Relate to those who are Suffering.* St. Louis, Missouri: Stephen Ministries, 2004.

_____. *A Time to Grieve: Book One.* Part of a series titled, *Journeying Through Grief.* St. Louis, MO): Stephen Ministries, 2004.

_____. *Experiencing Grief: Book Two. Journeying Through Grief.* St. Louis, MO: Stephen Ministries, 2004.

_____. *Finding Hope and Healing: Book Three. Journeying Through Grief.* St. Louis, MO: Stephen Ministries, 2004.

_____. *Rebuilding and Remembering: Book Four. Journeying Through Grief.* St. Louis, MO: Stephen Ministries, 2004.

Hernandez, Wil. *Henri Nouwen and Soul Care: A Ministry of Integration.* New York: Paulist Press, 2008.

_____. "Henri Nouwen on Presence in Absence". *Presence. An International Journal of Spiritual Direction.* Volume 18, Number 3, September 2012.

Higgins, Michael W. and Kevin Burns. *Genius Born of Anguish: The Life and Legacy of Henri Nouwen.* NY: Paulist Press, 2012.

Hiltner, Seward. *Pastoral Counseling.* Nashville: Abingdon, 1949.

Hitchcock, Mark. *55 Answers to Questions About Life After Death.* Sisters, OR: Multnomah Publishers, 2005.

Hodgson, Irene B., translator. *Through The Year with Oscar Romero: Daily Meditations.* Cincinnati, OH: St. Anthony Messenger Press, 1999, 2000.

Holder, Jennifer Sutton and Jann Aldredge-Clanton. *Parting: A Handbook for Spiritual Care Near the End of Life.* Chapel Hill: The University of North Carolina Press, 2004.

Holland, Debra. *The Essential Guide to Grief and Grieving.* NY: Alpha Books Penguin Group), 2011.

Holst, Lawrence, ed. *Hospital Ministry: The Role of the Chaplain Today.* NY: Crossroad, 1987.

Hoover, Brett C. *Comfort: An Atlas for the Body and Soul.* NY: Riverhead Books, 2011.

Hospice Foundation of America (HFA. www.hospicefoundation.org

Hunter, Rodney J., and Nancy J. Ramsay, eds. *Dictinary of Pastoral Care and Counseling.* Nashville: Abingdon, 2005.

Hutchison, Joyce and Joyce Rupp. *Now That You've Gone Home: Courage and Comfort for Times of Grief.* Notre Dame, IN: Ave Maria Press, 2009.

Irish Health Home Page: www.irishhealth.com. "Care of the Dying; End of Days." Accessed November 15, 2012.

Isso, John. *The Five Secrets You Must Discover Before You Die.* NY: MJF Books, 2008.

Jacobs, Martha R. *A Clergy Guide to End-of-Life Issues.* Cleveland: The Pilgrim Press, 2010.

Jacobson, Simon. *Toward A Meaningful Life: The Wisdom of the Rebbe Menachem Mendel Schneerson.* NY: Harper, 1995, 2002.

James, John W. and Frank Cherry. *The Grief Recovery Handbook: A Step-by-Step Program for Moving Beyond Loss.* NY: Harper & Row, 1988.

James, William. "The Varieties of Religious Experience: A Study in Human Nature." Gifford Lectures on Natural Religion delivered at Edinburgh in 1901-1902. NY: Longmans, Green and Company, 1928.

Jahnel, Christoph. *The Lutheran Church in El Salvador.* Tuscon, AZ: Christian Educational Services, 2004. Originally published in German as *Die Lutherische Kirche in El Salvador.*

Johnson, Elizabeth A. *Consider Jesus: Waves of Renewal in Christology.* NY: Crossroad, 1990, 2011.

_____. *Quest For the Living God: Mapping Frontiers in the Theology of God.* NY: Continuum International Publishing Group, 2007, 2011.

Johnson, Paul. *Jesus: A Biography from a Believer*. NY: Penguin Books, 2010.

Johnston, William. *Christian Zen*. NY: Harper & Row, Publishers, 1971.

Jones, Alan. *Soul Making: The Desert Way of Spirituality*. San Francisco: Harper, 1985.

Jonas, Robert A., ed. *The Essential Henri Nouwen*. Boston: Shambahala, 2009.

Kabat-Zinn, Jon. *Wherever You Go There You Are: Mindfulness Meditation In Everyday Life*. NY: Hyperion, 1994.

Kalina, Kathy. *Midwife For Souls: Spiritual Care for the Dying*. Boston: Pauline Books & Media,1993.

Kaltner, John. *Islam: What Non-Muslims Should Know*. Minneapolis: Fortress Press, 2003.

Kapleau, Philip. Compiled and edited. *The Three Pillars of Zen*. Boston: Beacon Press, 1965.

Kapleau, Philip. *The Zen of Living and Dying: A Practical and Spiritual Guide*. Boston: Shambhala, 1998.

Karnes, Barbara. *The Final Act of Living: Reflections of a Long-Time Hospice Nurse*. Depoe Bay, OR: Barbara Karnes Books, Inc., 2003.

_____. *Gone From My Sight: The Dying Experience*. Vancouver, WA: BKBooks, 1986, Revised, 2009.

Kelsey, Morton. *Dreams: A Way to Listen to God*. NY: Paulist Press, 1978.

_____. *Healing and Christianity*. NY: Harper & Row, Publishers, 1973.

Keating, Thomas. *Intimacy with God: An Introduction to Centering Prayer*. New York: A Crossroad Book, 2003.

Kelley, Patricia. *Companion to Grief: Finding Consolation When Someone You Love Has Died*. New York: Simon & Schuster, 1997.

Kessler, David. *The Needs of the Dying* (Previously published as *The Rights of the Dying*.) Quill, an imprint of Harper Collins Publishers, 1997, 2000.

Kidd, Sue Monk. *When the Heart Waits: Spiritual Direction for Life's Sacred Questions*. San Francisco: Harper & Row, Publishers, 1990.

_____. *God's Joyful Surprise: Finding Yourself Loved*. San Francisco: Harper & Row, Publishers, 1987.

Kirkwood, Neville A. *Pastoral Care in Hospitals*. Alexandria, Australia: E.J. Dwyer, Pty Ltd,1995.

_____. *A Hospital Handbook on Multiculturalism and Religion*. Newtown, Australia: Millennium Books, 1993.

King, Larry with Rabbi Irwin Katsof. *Powerful Prayers*. Los Angeles: Renaissance Books, 1998).

Kohut, Jeraldine and Kohut, Sylvester. *Hospice: Caring for the Terminally Ill*. Springfield, IL: Charles C. Thomas Publisher, 1984.

Kolodiejchuk, Brian, ed. *Mother Teresa. Come Be My Light. The Private Writings of the "Saint of Calcutta"*. NY: Doublebay, 2007.

Kok, James R. *90% of Helping is Just Showing Up*. Grand Rapids, MI: CRC Publications, 1996.

Kübler-Ross, Elisabeth. *On Death and Dying*. NY: Macmillan Publishing Co., Inc, 1969.

_____. *The Tunnel and the Light: Essential Insights on Living and Dying*. NY: Marlowe and Company, 1999.

Kübler-Ross, Elisabeth and Kessler, David. *Life Lessons*. NY: Scribner, 2000.

_____. *The Wheel of Life: A Memoir of Living and Dying*. NY: Touchstone, 1998.

_____. *Death: The Final Stage of Growth*. New York: Touchstone, 1975).

Kübler-Ross, Elisabeth and Kessler, David. *On Grief and Grieving: Finding the Meaning of Grief Through the Five Stages of Loss*. New York: Scribner, 2005.

Kuhl, David. *What Dying People Want: Practical Wisdom for the End of Life*. NY: Public Affairs, 2002.

Kushner, Harold S. *How Good Do We Have to Be?: A New Understanding of Guilt and Forgiveness*. Boston: Little, Brown and Company, 1996.

_____. *When Bad Things Happen to Good People*. NY: Avon Books/Division of the Hearst Corporation, 1981, 1983.

_____. *The Lord Is My Shepherd: Healing Wisdom of the Twenty-Third Psalm*. NY: Anchor Books. 2003.

Labacqz, Karen. *Ethics and Spiritual Care: A Guide for Pastors, Chaplains, and Spiritual Directors*. Nashville: Abingdon, 2000.

Lattanzi-Licht, Marcia with John J. Mahoney and Galen W. Miller. *The Hospice Choice: In Pursuit of a Peaceful Death*. NY: Fireside, 1998.

Laurie, Greg. *Hope for Hurting Hearts*. Dana Point, CA: Kerygma Publishing, 2008.

Leary, Lani. *No One Has To Die Alone: Preparing for a Meaningful Death*. New York: Atria Paperback, 2012).

Lee, Judith. *Before & After: What To Do When Someone Dies, A Clear Guide and Easy Reference for End of Life Decisions*. Los Angeles, CA: JEL Publishing, 2003).

Lewis, C.S. *A Grief Observed*. NY: HarperCollins Publishers, 1994).

Little, Paul E. *Know Why You Believe*. Updated and Expanded by Marie Little. Chariot Victor Publishing, 1967, 1999.

Lopez, Charles J, Jr. *Best Funeral Meditations*. Lima, OH: CSS Publishing Company, Inc, 1998). *"Jesus' Grief and Yours,"* 50-52; *"A Time To Be Born, A Time To Die,"* 53-55

Lopez, Steve. From the *Los Angeles* Times. "When Death is Certain, But Dignity is Not," November 12, 2011; "Not Ready to Die, But Prepared, December 4, 2011; "Pennsylvania Case a Chilling One For Death-With-Dignity Advocates," November 5, 2013; and "Struggling With The Stresses of Hospice Care," December 21, 2014.

Lopez, Donald S. *The Story of Buddhism: A Concise Guide to Its History & Teachings.* Harper San Francisco, 2001.

Lowenstein, Tom. *Buddhist Inspirations: Essential Philosophy, Truth, and Enlightenment.* London: Duncan Baird Publishers, 2005.

Lull, Timothy F. *My Conversations with Martin Luther.* Minneapolis: Augsburg, 1999.

Lull, Timothy F, ed. *Martin Luther's Basic Theological Writings.* Minneapolis: Fortress Press, 1989.

Lysaught, M. Therese & Joseph J. Kotva, Jr, eds. *On Moral Medicine: Theological Perspectives in Medical Ethics,* Third Edition. Grand Rapids, MI: William B. Eerdmans Publishing Company, 2012). See "The End of Life," 1027 - 1162.

Macquarrie, John. *Two Worlds Are Ours: An Introduction to Christian Mysticism.* Minneapolis: Fortress Press, 2005.

Madow, Leo. *Anger: How to Recognize and Cope With It.* NY: Charles Scribner's Sons, 1972.

Martin, James, SJ. *My Life with the Saints.* Chicago: Loyola Press, 2006.

_____. *Jesus: A Pilgrimage.* Harper One, 2014.

Martinson, Paul Varo, ed. *Islam: An Introduction for Christians.* Minneapolis: Augsburg Fortress, 1994.

Marty, Martin E. *A Cry of Absence: Reflections for the Winter of the Heart.* San Francisco: Harper & Row, Publishers, 1983.

_____. "Patient Presence: Attending to Death and Dying." *Bulletin.* Chicago: The Park Ridge Center for the Study of Health, Faith, and Ethics. May/June 2001.

Mathewes-Green, Frederica. *Praying the Jesus Prayer*. Brewster, MA: Paraclete Press, 2011.

Matlins, Stuart M. and Arthur J. Magida, eds. *How to Be a Perfect Stranger: The Essential Religious Etiquette Handbook*, 3rd Edition. Woodstock, VT: Skylight Paths Publishing, 2003.

Maugh, Thomas H II. "Former Dean of Yale Nursing School Was U.S. Hospice Pioneer." Florence S. Wald, 1917 – 2008. *Los Angeles Times*, Friday, November 14, 2008, B7, Obituaries.

May, Gerald G. *The Dark Night of the Soul*. Harper San Francisco, 2004.

_____. *Care of Mind, Care of Spirit*. Harper San Francisco, 1982, 1992.

McLaren, Brian D. *A Generous Orthodoxy*. Grand Rapids, Michigan: Zondervan, 2004.

McNees, Pat, ed. *Dying: A Book of Comfort: Healing Words on loss and Grief*. NY: Warner Books, 1996.

Meilaender, Gilbert. *Bioethics: A Primer for Christians*. Second Edition. Grand Rapids, Michigan: William B. Eerdmans Publishing Company, 2005).

Meisel, Anthony and M.L. del Mastro, Trans. *The Rule of St. Benedict*. NY: Image Books, 1975).

Menninger, Karl. *Whatever Became of Sin*. NY: Hawthorn Books, Inc., 1973.

Merton, Thomas. *New Seeds of Contemplation*. NY: A New Directions Book, 1972). Originally published by the Abbey of Gethsemani, Inc., 1961

_____. *Peace in the Post-Christian Era*. NY: Orbis Books, 2004.

_____. *Conjectures of a Guilty Bystander*. NY: Image Books, 1965.

_____. *Life and Holiness*. NY: Image Books, 1963.

_____. *Spiritual Direction and Meditation*. Collegeville, MN: The Liturgical Press, 1960.

_____. *Thoughts in Solitude*. New York: Farrar, Straus, 1958).

Miller, James E. with Susan C. Cutshall. *The Art of Being a Healing Presence: A Guide for Those in Caring Relationships*. Fort Wayne, IN: Willowgreen Publishing, 2001.

Mitchell, Kenneth R. and Anderson, Herbert. *All Our Losses, All Our Griefs*. Resources for Pastoral Care. Philadelphia: The Westminister Press, 1983.

Moody, Raymond A, Jr. *Life After Life: The Investigation of a Phenomenon – Survival of Bodily Death*. Harper San Francisco, 1975, 2001.

Moore, Thomas. *Care of the Soul: Guide for Cultivating Depth and Sacredness in Everyday Life*. NY: Harper Collins Publishers, 1992.

Morse, Melvin with Paul Perry. *Closer to the Light: Learning from Children's Near-Death Experiences*. NY: Villard Books, 1990.

Moynihan, Robert. *Pray for Me: The Life and Spiritual Vision of Pope Francis, First Pope From the Americas*. NY: Image, 2013.

Mrowiec, Katia, Michel Kubler, and Antoine Sfeir. *God Yahweh Allah: What Kids Want to Know: 100 Questions about Faith and Belief*. NY: Paulist Press, 2014.

Mundy, Linus. *Simply Merton: Wisdom From His Journals*. Cincinnati, OH: Franciscan Media, 2014.

Myers, Edward. *When Parents Die: A Guide for Adults*. Revised and Updated. NY: Penguin Books, 1986, 1997.

National Hospice and Palliative Care Organization NHPCO). www.nhpco.org

Neigh, Janet E. "The Evolution of Hospice." *Caring*, November, 2005.

Nelson, Valerie. "Dame Cicely Saunders, 87; Pioneered Modern System of Hospice Care." *Los Angeles Times*, Saturday, July 16, 2005, B 17, Obituaries.

Neuhaus, Richard John. *As I Lay Dying: Meditations Upon Returning.* NY: Basic Books, 2002).

Niebuhr, Reinhold. *The Nature and Destiny of Man: Gifford Lectures.* Two Volumes. NY: Charles Scribner's Sons, 1943, 1964.

Nolan, Steve. *Spiritual Care at the End of Life: The Chaplain as a 'Hopeful Presence'.* London: Jessica Kingsley Publishers, 2012.

Nouwen, Henri J.M. *Beyond the Mirror: Reflections on Death and Life.* NY: The Crossroad Publishing Company, 2013.

_____. *The Living Reminder: Service and Prayer in Memory of Jesus Christ.* New York: The Seabury Press, 1977.

_____. *The Wounded Healer: Ministry in Contemporary Society.* New York: Image Books, Doubleday, 1979).

_____. *Our Greatest Gift: A Meditation on Dying and Caring.* San Francisco: Harper, 1994.

_____. *The Return of the Prodigal Son: A Story of Homecoming.* NY: Image Books. Doubleday, 1992.

_____. *Home Tonight: Further Reflections on the Parable of the Prodigal Son.* NY: Doubleday, 2009.

_____. Compiled and edited by Timothy Jones. *Turn My Mourning Into Dancing: Finding Hope in Hard Times.* Nashville: Thomas Nelson, 2001.

Nuland, Sherwin B. *How We Die: Reflections on Life's Final Chapter.* NY: Vintage Books, 1993.

O'Rourke, Michelle. *Befriending Death: Henri Nouwen and a Spirituality of Dying.* New York: Orbis Books, 2009).

Ortberg, John. *If You Want To Walk On Water, You've Got To Get Out Of The Boat.* Grand Rapids, MI: Zondervan Publishing House, 2001.

Pagels, Elaine. *The Origin of Satan.* NY: Vintage Books. A Division of Random House, Inc., 1995, 1996.

Paget, Naomi K and Janet R. McCormack. *The Work of the Chaplain*. Valley Forge, PA: Judson Press, 2006.

Pelikan, Jaroslav. *Whose Bible Is It?: A History of the Scriptures Through the Ages*. NY: Viking, 2005.

_____. *Jesus Through the Centuries: His Place in the History of Culture*. New Haven, CT: Yale University Press, 1985.

Pennel, Joe E., Jr. *The Gift of Presence: A Guide to Helping Those Who Suffer*. Nashville, TN: Abingdon Press, 2009.

Person, Gretchen. *Psalms for Healing: Praying with Those in Need*. Minneapolis: Augsburg, 2001)

Peterson, Janice and Peterson, Carl. "End-of-Life Decisions and the Science-Theology Dialogue." *Lutheran Partners*, Volume 22, Number 2, July/August, 2006.

Piper, Don. *Heaven is Real*. Berkley Praise, NY: The Berkley Publishing Group, 2007.

Pirsig, Robert M. *Zen and the Art of Motorcycle Maintenance*. Harper Perennial Modern Classics, 2005.

Powell, Mark Allan. *Jesus as a Figure in History: How Modern Historians View the Man from Galilee*. Louisville, KY: Westminster John Knox Press, 1998.

Powell, Mark Allan. *Loving Jesus*. Minneapolis: Fortress Press, 2004.

Preaching on Death: An Ecumenical Resource. Silver Spring, MD: The Liturgical Conference, 1997.

Prend, Ashley Davis. *Transcending Loss: Understanding the Lifelong Impact of Grief and How to Make It Meaningful*. NY: Berkley Books, 1997.

Presence: An International Journal of Spiritual Direction. Spiritual Directors International, Bellevue, WA.

Providence Trinity Care Hospice. "What to Expect. Helping a Loved One Through the Process of Dying." No Date. www.trinitycarehospice.org

Pruyser, Paul W. *The Minister As Diagnostician: Personal Problems in Pastoral Perspective.* Philadelphia: The Westminster Press, 1976.

_____. *A Dynamic Psychology of Religion.* NY: Harper & Row, Publishers, 1968.

_____. *Between Belief and Unbelief.* NY: Harper & Row, Publishers, 1974)

Ramsay, Nancy J., ed. *Pastoral Care and Counseling: Redefining the Paradigms.* Nashville: Abingdon, 2005.

Ramsay, Nancy J. *Pastoral Diagnosis: A Resource for Ministries of Care and Counseling.* Minneapolis: Augsburg Fortress, 1998.

Ramsey, Paul. *The Patient as Person: Explorations in Medical Ethics.* Second Edition. Yale University Press, 2002).

_____. *Basic Christian Ethics.* Louisville: Westminster John Knox Press, 1950.

Rando, Therese A. *How To Go On Living When Someone You Love Dies.* New York: Bantam Books, 1991.

Rando. Therese A. *Treatment of Complicated Mourning.* Champaign, IL: Research Press, 1993.

Ratzinger, Joseph. (Pope Benedict XVI) *Jesus of Nazareth.* The Infancy Narratives, 2012.

Reimer, Lawrence D. and James T. Wagner. *The Hospital Handbook: A Practical Guide to Hospital Visitation.* Second Edition. Harrisburg, PA: Morehouse Publishing, 1984, 1988.

Rinpoche, Sogyal. *The Tibetan Book of Living and Dying.* Revised and Updated Edition. Patrick Gaffney and Andrew Harvey, eds. Harper San Francisco, A Division of Harper Collins Publishers, 2002.

Rinpoche, Guru. *The Tibetan Book of the Dead: The Great Liberation Through Hearing in the Bardo.* Translated with commentary by Francesca Fremantle and Chogyam Trungpa. Boston: Shambhala, 1987).

Roberts, Arthur O. *Exploring Heaven: What Great Christian Thinkers Tell Us About Our Afterlife with God.* Harper San Francisco, 2003.

Robinson, Gene. *God Believes in Love.* NY: Alfred A. Knopf, 2012.

Robinson, George. *Essential Torah: A Complete Guide to the Five Books of Moses.* NY: Schocken Books, 2006),

Rogers, Fred. *You Are Special: Words of Wisdom from America's Most Beloved Neighbor.* NY: Viking, 1994.

_____. *Life's Journeys According to Mister Rogers: Things to Remember Along the Way.* NY: Hyperion, 2005.

Rolheiser, Ronald. *The Holy Longing: The Search for a Christian Spirituality.* New York: Doubleday, 1999.

Rolheiser, Ronald. *Prayer: Our Deepest Longing.* Cincinnati, OH: Franciscan Media, 2013.

Rohr, Richard. *Everything Belongs: The Gift of Contemplative Prayer.* Revised & Updated Edition. NY: The Crossroad Publishing Company,1999, 2003.

_____. *Falling Upward: A Spirituality for the Two Halves of Life.* San Francisco: Jossey-Bass, 2011.

_____. *Immortal Diamond: The Search for Our True Self.* San Francisco: Jossey-Bass, 2013.

_____. *Silent Compassion: Finding God in Contemplation.* Cincinnati, OH: Franciscan Media, 2014.

_____. *Things Hidden: Scripture as Spirituality.* Cincinnati, OH: Franciscan Media, 2008.

_____. *Job and the Mystery of Suffering: Spiritual Reflections.* NY: The Crossroad Publishing Company, 1996, 2011.

Romero, Oscar. *The Violence of Love: The Pastoral Wisdom of Archbishop Oscar Romero.* Compiled and Translated by James R. Brockman, S.J. San Francisco: Harper & Row, Publishers,1988.

Ruffing, Janet K. *Spiritual Direction: Beyond the Beginnings.* New York: Paulist Press, 2000.

Rumford, Douglas J. *What About Heaven & Hell?: The Bible's Answers to Your Questions about the Afterlife.* Wheaton, IL: Tyndale House Publishers, Inc., 2000.

St. Christopher's Hospice. www.stchristophers.org.uk.

Sanders. E.P. *The Historical Figure of Jesus.* NY: Penguin Books, 1993.

Saltzman, Russell E. *Speaking of the Dead: When We All Fall Down.* Delhi, NY: American Lutheran Publicity Bureau, 2014.

Sankar, Andrea. *Dying At Home: A Family Guide for Caregiving.* NY: Bantam Books,1991,1995.

Schneider, Edward, ed. *Questions About the Beginning of Life: Christian Appraisals of Seven Bioethical Issues.* Minneapolis: Augsburg Publishing House, 1985.

Sesame Street. "When Families Grieve: A Special Guide For Parents and Caregivers." DVD with booklet in English & Spanish. 2010, www.sesamestreet.org/grief

Siegel, Bernie S. *Love, Medicine & Miracles: Lessons Learned About Self-Healing from a Surgeon's Experience with Exceptional Patients.* NY: Harper & Row, Publishers,1986.

_____. *Peace, Love and Healing: Bodymind Communication & the Path to Self-Healing: An Exploration.* NY: Harper & Row, Publishers, 1989.

Simon, Art. *Rediscovering the Lord's Prayer.* Minneapolis: Augsburg Books, 2005.

Simundson, Daniel J. *Where is God in my Suffering: Biblical Responses to Seven Searching Questions.* Minneapolis: Augsburg Publishing House, 1983.

_____. *Where is God in My Praying: Biblical Responses to Eight Searching Questions.* Minneapolis: Augsburg Publishing House, 1986.

———. *Faith Under Fire: How the Bible Speaks to Us in Times of Suffering.* Harper San Francisco, 1991).

Smith, Douglas C. *Caregiving: Hospice-Proven Techniques for Healing Body and Soul.* NY: Wiley Publishing, Inc., 1997.

Smith, Huston. *The World's Religions: Our Great Wisdom Traditions.* Revised & Updated Edition of The Religions of Man. Harper San Francisco, 1958, 1991.

Smith, Huston. *Why Religion Matters: The Fate of the Human Spirit in an Age of Disbelief.* Harper San Francisco, 2001.

Smith, Huston and Philip Novak. *Buddhism: A Concise Introduction.* Harper San Francisco, 2003.

Sparks, Allister & Mpho Tutu. *Tutu Authorized.* Foreword by Bono. Introduction by His Holiness the Fourteenth Dalai Lama. Harper One, 2011.

Speerstra, Karen and Herbert Anderson. *The Divine Art of Dying: How To Live Well While Dying.* Divine Arts, 2014.

Spong, John Shelby. *Jesus for the Non-Religious.* Harper One, 2007.

Staudacher, Carol. *Beyond Grief: A Guide for Recovering from the Death of a Loved One.* Oakland, CA: New Harbinger Publications, Inc., 1987.

Strobel, Lee. *The Case for the Real Jesus.* Grand Rapids, Michigan: Zondervan, 2007.

Stoddard, Sandol. *The Hospice Movement: A Better Way of Caring for the Dying.* NY: Stein and Day Publishers, 1978.

Sweeney, Mary Therese CSJ and Eileen McNerney, CSJ. *A Bold and Humble Love: Journey of Grace.* Sisters of St. Joseph of Orange, 1912-2012. Orange, CA: Sisters of St. Joseph of Orange, 2012). www.csjorange.org.

Talbot, John Michael. *The Jesus Prayer: A Cry for Mercy, A Path of Renewal.* Downers Grove, IL: IVP Books, 2013.

Tatelbaum, Judy. *The Courage to Grieve.* NY: Harper & Row, Publishers, 1980.

The Oxford Dictionary of Quotations. Second Edition. London: Oxford University Press, 1953.

The Tibetan Book of the Dead. First Complete Translation. Introductory Commentary by His Holiness The Dalai Lama. Penguin Books, 2005.

Thomas à Kempis. *Imitation of Christ*. NY: Image Books/Doubleday, 1955.

Tickle, Phyllis. *Emergence Christianity: What It Is, Where It Is Going, and Why It Matters*. Grand Rapids, MI: Baker Books, 2012.

Tippett, Krista. *Speaking of Faith: Why Religion Matters – and How To Talk About It*. NY: Penguin Books, 2007)

Toole, Mary M. *Handbook for Chaplains: Comfort My People*. NY: Paulist Press, 2006.

Twerski, Abraham J. *When Do the Good Things Start?: A Therapist looks at Life's Ups and Downs*. Peanuts Cartoons by Charles M. Schulz. NY: Topper Books, 1988.

Vest, Norvene, ed. *Still Listening: New Horizons in Spiritual Direction*. Harrisburg, PA: Morehouse Publishing, 2000.

Wallis, Jim. *The (Un)Common Good: How the Gospel Brings Hope to a World Divided*. Grand Rapids, MI: Brazos Press, 2013, 2014.

Walsch, Neale Donald. *What God Wants: A Compelling Answer to Humanity's Biggest Question*. NY: Atria Books, 2005.

Walsch, Neale Donald. *The Complete Conversations with God: An Uncommon Dialogue*. Contains the entire text of Book 1, Book 2, and Book 3. NY: G.P. Putnam's Sons, 1995, 2002, 2003, 2005.

Wangerin, Walter, Jr. *Mourning into Dancing*. Grand Rapids, MI: Zondervan Publishing House, 1992.

Weaver, Andrew J. and Stone, Howard W, editors. *Reflections on Grief and Spiritual Growth*. Nashville: Abingdon Press, 2005.

Weckman, George. *My Brothers' Place: An American Lutheran Monastery*. Lawrenceville, VA: Brunswick Publishing Corporation, 1992.

Wennberg, Robert N. *Terminal Choices: Euthanasia, Suicide, and the Right to Die*. Grand Rapids, MI: William B. Eerdmans Publishing Company, 1989.

Wentzel, Kenneth B. *To Those Who Need it Most, Hospice Means Hope*. Boston: Charles River Books. 1981.

Westberg, Granger E. *Good Grief*. Minneapolis: Fortress Press, 2011), 50th Anniversary Edition.

Westberg, Jane with Jill Westberg McNamara. *Gentle Rebel: The Life and Work of Granger Westberg, Pioneer in Whole Person Care*. Memphis, TN: Church Health, 2015.

Wilken, Robert L. *The Land Called Holy: Palestine In Christian History & Thought*. New Haven: Yale University Press, 1992.

Wilkinson, Philip & Philip, Neil. *Mythology*. NY: Metro Books, 2007.

_____. *Religions*. NY: Metro Books, 2008.

Willard, Dallas. *Hearing God: Developing a Conversational Relationship with God*. Downers Grove, IL: InterVarsity Press, 1984, 1993, 1999). NOTE: Previously published under the title In Search of Guidance in 1984 by Regal Books.

Williams, Rowan. *Where God Happens: Discovering Christ In One Another*. Foreword by Desmond Tutu. Boston: New Seeds, 2005.

Wolfelt, Alan D. *The Journey Through Grief: Reflections on Healing*. Second Edition. Fort Collins, CO: Companion Press, 2003.

Wolpe, Rabbi David. *Making Loss Matter: Creating Meaning in Difficult Times*. NY: Riverhead Books, 1999.

Worden, J. William. *Grief Counseling and Grief Therapy: A Handbook for the Mental Health Practitioner*. Second Edition. New York: Springer Publishing Company, 1991.

_____. *Children and Grief: When a Parent Dies*. NY: The Guilford Press, 1996.

Wright, N. T. *Jesus and the Victory of God: Christian Origins and the Question of God*, Volume 2. Minneapolis: Fortress Press, 1996.

_____. *Simply Christian: Why Christianity Makes Sense*. San Francisco: HarperOne, 2006.

Wright, Vinita Hampton. *Prayers Across the Centuries: Abraham, Jesus, St. Augustine, Martin Luther, Susanna Wesley*. Wheaton, IL: Harold Shaw Publishers, 1993.

Yancey, Philip. *Reaching for the Invisible God*. Grand Rapids, MI: Zondervan, 2000.

Author Biography

The Rev. Charles Joseph Lopez, Jr, PhD was born and raised in Chicago. He has served over 40 years in ministry (September 28,1975 Ordination): 27 years as a Lutheran parish pastor in NJ, PA, CA, and Bogota, Colombia, South America; pastoral psychotherapist (17 years in NJ & PA); and 13 years as hospice chaplain with Providence Trinity Care Hospice (part of Providence Little Company of Mary Medical Center, Torrance, CA). He is ordained and serves as clergy member of the Pacifica Synod of the Evangelical Lutheran Church in America (ELCA). He has certificates in spiritual direction (2006) and bioethics (2013) from Loyola Marymount University, Los Angeles. He is a member with the Association for Death Education & Counseling (ADEC), Association of Professional Chaplains (APC), and Academy of Parish Clergy (APC) and has received scholarships from the Lutheran World Federation; Aid Association for Lutherans; Growth in Excellence in Ministry (ELCA); and Loyola Marymount University (Bioethics). Charley is listed in *Who's Who in Religion* as well as *Who's Who in America*. He is listed on LinkedIn, ZoomInfo, and Facebook. He loves baseball, basketball, cycling, traveling and classical music. He adores all kinds of palm trees, flowers, and oceans. He follows Chicago sports, especially the Cubs, White Sox, Bulls, Blackhawks and Bears!! He is the proud owner of one share with the Green Bay Packers!!

www.ingramcontent.com/pod-product-compliance
Lightning Source LLC
LaVergne TN
LVHW021559070426
835507LV00014B/1869